POLAR IN

Theory, Culture & Society

Theory, Culture & Society caters for the resurgence of interest in culture within contemporary social science and the humanities. Building on the heritage of classical social theory, the book series examines ways in which this tradition has been reshaped by a new generation of theorists. It also publishes theoretically informed analyses of everyday life, popular culture, and new intellectual movements.

EDITOR: Mike Featherstone, *Nottingham Trent University*

SERIES EDITORIAL BOARD
Roy Boyne, *University of Durham*
Mike Hepworth, *University of Aberdeen*
Scott Lash, *Goldsmiths College, University of London*
Roland Robertson, *University of Pittsburgh*
Bryan S. Turner, *University of Cambridge*

THE TCS CENTRE
The Theory, Culture & Society book series, the journals *Theory, Culture & Society* and *Body & Society*, and related conference, seminar and postgraduate programmes operate from the TCS Centre at Nottingham Trent University. For further details of the TCS Centre's activities please contact:

Centre Administrator
The TCS Centre, Room 175
Faculty of Humanities
Nottingham Trent University
Clifton Lane, Nottingham, NG11 8NS, UK
e-mail: tcs@ntu.ac.uk
web: http//tcs@ntu.ac.uk

Recent volumes include:

Digital Aesthetics
Sean Cubitt

Facing Modernity
Ambivalence, Reflexivity and Morality
Barry Smart

Culture as Praxis
Zygmunt Bauman

Radical Conservatism and the Future of Politics
Göran Dahl

Spaces of Culture
City, Nation, World
Mike Featherstone and Scott Lash

Love and Eroticism
edited by Mike Featherstone

POLAR INERTIA

Paul Virilio

Translated by Patrick Camiller

SAGE Publications
London · Thousand Oaks · New Delhi

English translation © Sage Publications 2000

First published in English 2000

Originally published as *L'Inertie polaire*, © Christian Bourgois 1990

This translation is published with financial support from the French Ministry of Culture

Published in association with *Theory, Culture & Society*, School of Health, Social and Policy Studies, University of Teesside

 SAGE Publications Ltd
6 Bonhill Street
London EC2A 4PU

SAGE Publications Inc
2455 Teller Road
Thousand Oaks, California 91320

SAGE Publications India Pvt Ltd
32, M-Block Market
Greater Kailash-I
New Delhi 110 048

British Library Cataloguing in Publication data
A catalogue record for this book is available from the British Library
ISBN 0-7619-5802-9
ISBN 0-7619-5803-7 (pbk)

Library of Congress catalog record available

Typeset by Type Study, Scarborough, North Yorkshire
Printed in Great Britain by Redwood Books, Trowbridge, Wiltshire

For Sophie

CONTENTS

1

INDIRECT LIGHT

Light is the name of the shadow of the living light.

Bernard de Clairvaux

I still remember my astonishment, ten years ago, when I saw video screens replacing mirrors on Paris Metro platforms.

Soon after 1968, it is true, surveillance cameras had appeared at the entrances to the *grandes écoles* and universities, and this new equipment was also used to keep watch on the boulevards and major junctions of the capital.[1] Today, I am astonished once again when I see the lens of a micro-camera rising above the keypad that gives coded access to a block of flats. Evidently entry phones are no longer enough to do the job of the old concierges.

As an electro-optical substitute, *videoscopy* seems to come into its own with this role of indirectly lighting a domestic environment for which electric light, a direct form analogous to daylight, is no longer sufficient. Rapid miniaturization is indeed making the video camera and its monitor more and more akin to a *warning light* that comes on to let us see who is here or who is there.

Even the old 35 mm cine-camera has had its eyepiece viewfinder replaced to advantage with a screen that actually displays the recorded images.

How can one fail to see here the essential characteristic of video technology: not a more or less up-to-the-minute 'representation' of an event, but *live presentation of a place* or an electro-optical environment – the result, it would seem, of *putting reality on waves* by means of electro-magnetic physics?

It is logical, then, to find here not any performance space, any 'screening room', but only a *control room*.

In furnishing the image of a place, videography does not itself require any 'space' except for its supporting camera and monitor, themselves integrated – or dissolved, as it were – into other equipment having nothing to do with 'artistic' televisual or cinematic representation.

Just as one is not bothered by the dials and lights on a car dashboard or by the lighting in a shop window, so one is not really troubled by the 'broadcasting' or 'diffusion' area of a video camera. That area is solely *what is lit up*, and not the 'theatre' or site of a cinema performance screened at some distant location.

So great is the difference between video observation, cinema and television that the TV set has itself been overtaken through the incorporation of monitors into the most ordinary domestic equipment – for example, the 'electro-optical porter' that makes people visible as the entry phone only made them audible.

The whole debate on the crisis of cinemas, on the miniaturization of public film theatres, will no doubt soon be repeated in relation to private homes and the 'living room', where the TV set is still often located. For the emancipation of the screen will involve not only its sudden expansion into the giant open-air Jumbotron or Olympic stadium screen, but also its *compression* into a scattered array of ordinary objects unconnected with televisual performance or information.

Who still cares about the electrical wires in domestic appliances? Who tomorrow will care about the optical fibres built into commonly used materials or equipment?

Alongside the *broadcasting* of current political or artistic events, video 'illuminates' us about phenomena instantaneously *transmitted* across varying distances and thus becomes itself a new type of tele-topographic 'site' or location. (Is there not already talk of 'neighbourhood television'?) Just as Edison's invention of the electric light-bulb caused daytime places to appear at night, the new electro-optical lamp causes places to become visible amid generally invisible surroundings. As the site of the non-site of instantaneous transmission (at varying distances), it effects a kind of commutation of perceptible appearances similar to that which occurs in para-optic perception and quite unrelated to ordinary mass-media communication.[2]

Thus, alongside the well-known effects of 'telescopy' and 'microscopy', which have revolutionized our perception of the world since the seventeenth century, it will not be long before the repercussions of 'videoscopy' make themselves felt through the constitution of an instantaneous, interactive 'space-time' that has nothing in common with the topographical space of geographical or even simply geometrical distance.

Whereas theatrical or cinematic *mise en scène* involves the spatio-temporal organization of stage action or film narrative in an area used for public performances, and whereas, to a lesser degree, production for television requires a private stage or broadcasting area (the rooms of a private home), this no longer applies to video transmission. For 'cine-videography' solely consists in the *commutation* of more or less distant and disjointed appearances, and also in the commutation of interactive actors at varying distances. Commutation of the emission and reception of the video signal, at the monitoring terminal, indicates the *mutation-commutation* of distances (topology) into *power* (tele-topology), that is, into light energy as the union of relativist cinema and wave optics.

The present crisis of cinemas is not therefore mainly due to an increase in domestic film-viewing; rather, it expresses a crisis in the idea of representation linked to rapid spread of the 'live' dimension. The live 'real-time' spectacle is a result of the development of videoscopy, not only in people's homes, but here, there and everywhere, in the very body of the various pieces of equipment in which it began to be incorporated nearly twenty years ago. (The most striking example is the weaving of optical fibres into composite materials.) The crisis, then, is a crisis of *delayed* broadcasting as such, so that electro-optical imaging techniques now impose the idea – or, to be more precise, the 'ideography' – of a veritable presentation of places and milieux, a 'presentation' which corresponds, on a human scale, to what telescopic presentation meant for astronomy or microscopic presentation for the innermost properties of materials.

Video is no more the eighth art than cinema was the seventh. The crisis affecting cinema box-office, rival TV channels but also what is called art video stems from the fact that, ever since the beginnings of photography and cinema, as well as of radio and television, the showing of *events* or entertainments has been more important than *the lighting up of the places* where they happen. Notwithstanding Edison, Marey, the Lumière Brothers, Vertov and a few others, the fun of the fair nearly always took priority over illumination (and did so more than ever with the coming of television), but the appearance of an *active optics* has suddenly replaced the feats of passive optics (of glass and other transparent lens material) in the organization of perceptible reality. This startling new *presence of tele-reality* transforms the nature of both the object and the subject of traditional representation, so that *pictures of places have now taken over from the 'picture houses'* where performances used to occur. Only the theatre, thanks to its unity of time and place, still escapes the transmutations of electro-optical lighting whose immediacy excludes 'unity of place' for the sole benefit of 'unity of time', albeit of a *real time* which seriously affects the space of real things.

In fact, alongside the 'radio-activity' of emission and reception, with its 'electro-acoustic high fidelity', there is now what might be called the 'opto-activity' of videoscopic commutation, with all the problems of 'electro-optical high definition' that this implies.

* * *

When there is talk in Toulouse and elsewhere of the imminent introduction of neighbourhood television (*télé locale*), people do not realize that they are borrowing a term from videoscopy or, in the case of a cabled city, from a 'videography' that allows the town to *see itself* and to *make itself visible* – that is, to become its own 'production', its own film.

The city of Rennes, for example, has a plan for 'electronic public lighting' to boost the political and economic existence of the urban area – hence the requirement for a municipal tele-noticeboard and the inevitable telesales that will replace the local press with one huge cathode shop-window. But is this not already how things are with the more limited proximity of objects and places in our everyday environment, with the Metro video terminals, the company's closed-circuit television, or the shops that are able to see the faces of window-gazers? And that is nothing compared with 'wall-socket' cameras and 'light-bulb' monitors built into ordinary objects, much as the microphone and loudspeaker were earlier incorporated into alarm-clock, tape recorder or walkman, or the digital displays of quartz watches were implanted into pen tops, cigarette lighters and all manner of other objects. In the realm of videoscopic display, however, commutation is different. 'Geographically close' television and 'geometrically close' video are *parasitic* upon clear perception of the here and now: they interpenetrate and interchange places *tele-topologically*, thanks to sudden 'live' revelation of the 'space-speed' at present supplanting the space-time of our ordinary activities. Merging with para-optical illumination, the upper speed limit of live transmission defines itself as indirect lighting at the speed of the video signal.

It is often claimed in the West that miniaturization, like giant screens, is a Japanese gadget. But this is not true. What is happening in image physics is also happening in astrophysics, where the Hubble space telescope is soon to come into operation with *adaptive optics*, that is, with image correction that depends on the computer's capacity and not just on the properties of the lens.

Screen and picture size therefore have nothing to do with it; the dimensions of the object are no longer what counts. For now the cathode screen displays *spatial distance that changes before our eyes into luminous energy, into illumination power.*

As a new kind of distance – the 'light (zero sign) of the new physics'[3] – suddenly takes the place of the customary distances of time (positive sign) and space (negative sign), every surface of whatever size has an objective existence only in and through the interface of an observation which, instead of just being the visible result of direct solar or electric lighting, is due to indirect lighting by the radio-electrical field of a Hertzian system or an optical fibre cable.

What we see for the *maximal surface* of the globe subjected to constant scrutiny by military, meteorological and other satellites is also true for the *minimal surfaces* of objects and places subjected to the intense lighting of videoscopy. In fact, a mysterious 'tele-bridge' is established between an ever-growing number of surfaces, from the largest to the most minute, in a kind of sound-and-image feedback which triggers for us observers a (video-geographical or video-geometrical) 'tele-presence' or 'tele-reality' essentially expressed by the concept of real time.

What Einstein's 'point of view theory' taught us in 1905 about the relativity of extension and duration – that is, the inseparable face-to-face meeting of observer and observed surfaces, a relativist interface without which extension has no objective dimension – is *visibly* confirmed by instantaneous video feedback in which the electro-optical environment wins out over the classical 'ecological' environment. A kind of 'electronic meteorology' thereby asserts itself without which the meteorology of the earth's atmosphere would soon become incomprehensible. At a time when the major US television channels ABC, CBS and NBC are faring worse and worse, Ted Turner's live news channel, CNN, is planning a 'News Hound' service for a million subscribers with video equipment. 'That's a million opportunities for us,' Earl Casey, the man in charge of this future interactive system, said recently, '*a million witnesses able to provide us with pictures*; all we'll have to do is select.'

In the military sphere, eminently strategic research into *stealth* aircraft points in the same direction. While a complex environment of electro-magnetic detection is established at global level, active research is being pursued into ways of escaping 'radio-electrical sight' through special new materials such as the PBZ super-polymer, which is said to be capable of avoiding detection by radar waves. At the same time, however, aeronautical producers are asked to embed in the same material optical fibres capable of sounding, or permanently illuminating, the dense cells and organs driving the combat aircraft.

For the philosopher Schopenhauer, the world was its representation. For the 'video-maker' or electronics expert, we may say, matter is becoming its presentation – direct and external 'presentation' and, at the same time, internal and indirect presentation, the object or instrument becoming not only present to the naked eye but remotely present or '*tele-present*'.

This *physical non-separability* of outside and inside, near and distant, is also exemplified by the road-haulage industry and by the development of 'star' publicity. Thus the American Geostar company, and soon its European counterpart Locstar, are due in the near future to place the first piece of their 'Radio Determination Satellite Service' in orbit. Thanks to this surveillance system, the headquarters of a haulage company will know at any moment the geographical position of each of its vehicles, a geo-stationary navigation satellite enabling it to monitor and control movements. We can see why the magazine *Match* has just had its logo drawn in the Chott Djerid (dear to Bill Viola) of central Tunisia, suddenly turning the desert into a kind of screen, as all the continental and oceanic surfaces have become for the gaze of orbiting satellites.

But this ceaseless *rapprochement* of above and below would not be complete if, after the nadir, we left out the zenith – that is, the minor miracle of high-orbit billposting which is Coca-Cola's plan to leave its indelible mark on our nightly firmament.[4]

Once again we notice the decline of the sites of representation and projection. Theatre, stage or screen become simply *the sky and the ground*, all the surfaces from the smallest to the largest that are exposed, nay, *overexposed*, to the inquisitive gaze of automatic instant-relay cameras – surfaces or, more exactly, 'interfaces' which have objective existence only as a result of videoscopic examination by live-relay recording material. *This 'real-time' tele-reality is supplanting the reality of the real-space presence* of objects and places, now overridden by electro-magnetic paths.

* * *

For Einstein, what distinguished a correct theory from a wrong theory was only the length of time for which it remained valid: a few years or decades for the former, a few moments or days for the latter. Is it not perhaps the same with the duration of images, with the difference between the 'real-time' and the 'delayed-time' image?

In the end, the whole problem of 'tele-reality' (or 'tele-presence', if that seems preferable) hinges on this same question of the validity of a short duration; the real value of the *object* or *subject* instantaneously present at a distance entirely depends upon the *passage*, that is, the speed, of its image, the speed of light of contemporary electro-optics. It is the same with 'remote' or 'tele' action, thanks to the capacity for instantaneous interaction in telemetry. The *opto-activity* of the online image is similar to the *radio-activity* of a device that handles objects at a distance (remote-controlled vehicles, transfer machines, various kinds of instrument).[5]

This advent of the real 'passage' to the detriment of the real object and subject – a phenomenon so indicative of the primacy of image over thing resulting from the new supremacy of real time over real space – clearly reveals the wave character of reality. For the sudden *commutation of perceptible appearances* is ultimately only the herald of a general derealization resulting from the new illumination of perceptible reality – a reality not just 'apparent' as before, but 'transparent' or, to be even more precise, *trans-apparent*.

There is a fusion/confusion of transmitted appearances and immediate appearances, with indirect lighting capable of soon supplanting direct lighting – not only, of course, artificial electric lighting but above all natural lighting, with the revolutionary changes in perception that this implies. The advent of passage as instantaneous and ubiquitous is thus the advent of *time light*, the intensive time of electro-optics which is supplanting for ever traditional passive optics.

We can bet, though, that the status of reality will not long resist this sudden illumination of places, happenings and events. For while improvements in the *spatial* definition of optical camera lenses have made it easier to see contrasts and increased the luminosity of the habitual image, recent improvements in the *temporal* definition of filming and electronic transmission procedures have increased the clarity and resolution of videoscopic images. Thus, audiovisual speed primarily helps us to see and to hear, or, in other words, *to move forward in the light of real time*, as automobile speed helped us to move forward in the real space of an area of land.

The greater 'transparency' of high-speed communications (TGV, supersonic aircraft, etc.) is thus compounded by the sudden (electro-optical and acoustic) trans-appearance of the means of information and telecommunication. High fidelity and high image definition serve greatly to modify the nature of the (acoustic or visual) relief, which in the end comes down to the greater or lesser reality of the things perceived, a spatio-temporal relief conditioning our apprehension of the world and of present time. Since the eye interprets any change in luminous intensity as a change in form, the light (direct or indirect, natural or artificial) produces not only the colour of objects and places but also their relief. Hence the importance of research into high definition of the image, definition at once spatial and temporal of a video signal capable of achieving for visual space what high fidelity of the radio signal has already done for the stereophony of sound volumes: *a veritable stereo-optics integrated into the domestic environment.*

Thus, just as star-filming techniques continually improve the image resolution of remote detection satellites, so the constant improvement of TV picture definition increases not the electrical transparency of the local environment (as at the beginning of the century, with the electrification of town and country), but the *electro-optical trans-appearance* of the *global* environment. This means the emergence of a new kind of 'relief' or audiovisual volume applying to the totality of transmitted appearances, a 'stereo-videoscopy' whose significance at macroscopic level is similar to that of the sudden breakthrough of electron microscopy in disclosing the infinitely small. In order to see, one is no longer content to dispel the shadows of surrounding darkness; the commutation of appearances can also remove the obstacle of extension, the opacity of great distance, thanks to ruthlessly penetrative videoscopic equipment that is analogous to the most powerful of floodlights. As the electro-optical *faux jour* of indirect public lighting dawns, as the real is put on air as the figurative, a new artificial light now complements electric lighting in much the same way that electric lighting once filled in for daylight.

At 1.32 p.m. local time, on 26 October 1987, a Titan–34D rocket launched a KH11 satellite from Vandenberg air base in California. *From its polar orbit covering the whole planet*, this satellite is able, at any moment of its ceaseless electronic scanning, to zoom in, spin round and transmit pictures in the form of electronic impulses. The average life of this military light is thirty-six months.

* * *

The invention of cinema can no more be separated from the invention of searchlights than it can from that of snapshot photography. Did not Thomas Edison, inventor of the incandescent lamp in 1879, work on the kinetograph a few years later? As to Louis Lumière, at the Universal Exhibition of 1900 the French Navy lent him its most powerful searchlight to project his films on a large screen, in the famous Gallery of Machines. And in 1948, shortly before his death, the pioneer of the cinema was still working to improve lighthouses for the Navy.

Today, the projection of wide film onto planetarium domes is only possible with a 15 kW xenon lamp initially designed to illuminate NASA's rocket-launching sites.

Finally, in 1969 when the astronauts returned from the Apollo 11 lunar mission, the President of the United States ordered all the coastal cities to be lit up, as ordinary lampposts are lit up in the evening along marine boulevards. This was meant as a homage not only to the conquerors of the moon but also to the sudden power of public lighting to reveal man's presence to the farthest reaches of the atmosphere.

If one thinks of the illumination of theatres and palace festivities in the age of Louis XIV or the introduction of electric street lighting at the end of the last century, it is clear that the history of public spectacle has been inseparable from the history of light – from fireworks through the diorama of Daguerre (a decorator at the Paris Opera and the Ambigu Comique) to the *son et lumière* displays of recent times. The birth of the cinema was itself inseparable from the development of artificial light, the famous 'arc lamps' being necessary both for the shooting of films in studios and for their screening in public theatres.

The other revealing aspect of this sudden extension of transparency has more to do with police requirements, for lighting makes the streets safer and so prolongs the time for commercial enrichment. Already in 1667, long before the days of video surveillance, Police Lieutenant La Reynie issued a famous ordinance that led to Paris's world reputation as the *ville lumière*. Then came the electrification of town and country in the early twentieth century, an undertaking rather like the present laying of cable to carry video along optical fibres throughout the big conglomerations. But now the shift concerns the very nature of the light, which is no longer just artificial but *indirect*, differing from direct light as much as candlelight once did from the light of the stars.

We should also mention here the *light-intensification* camera (or binoculars) currently used by the Army to see in the middle of the night over considerable distances. Often replacing infrared systems, this 'low-light television' amplifies the surrounding light, however weak, by nearly a hundred thousand times. In a way it is similar to a particle accelerator. Consisting of a tube placed in a powerful and continuous electrical field, the film camera has successive levels of photon acceleration which increase accordingly the luminosity of the final image; the accelerated light particles strike a screen with a phosphorus film at the other end of the tube, causing each particle of the film to glow. Lately this kind of indirect lighting equipment has started to be used by the German and British police, especially for football stadium surveillance.

In fact, where the *real time* of live television broadcasting prevails over the real space of a land actually crossed, the mere distinction between natural and artificial light is no longer enough; one has to add the difference in kind between *direct light*, natural or artificial, and *indirect light*, for electro-optical lighting now replaces electrical lighting as the latter once did the rising of the day.

And this is while we wait for the active optics of computer graphics to achieve its next feat: that is, the coupling of the passive optics of cameras with a computer capable of rectifying the transmitted image as only glass lenses used to do. *Digital optics* will then succeed analogue optics, as the latter once cleverly complemented the ocular optics of the human gaze.

As the image is the most sophisticated form of information, it is logical to expect that advances in computing will also end in the deployment of this indirect light: *digital light* this time, capable of piercing reality's shadows and of most realistically conveying an unknown transparency, such as fractal geometry already makes possible, with digital zoom effects that are nothing other than computer-generated *synthetic lighting*. The passages and their 'trans-appearance' signal the innermost constituents of the form-image, *shape of that which has no shape, image of that which has no image* (Lao-Tse) – a figure for the dynamic of emptiness, similar to the void of sub-atomic physics for which Oriental thought long ago paved the way.

But let us return to the city, the 'light-city' that has been home to all historical illuminations from the Fire of Rome through the pyrotechnics of the Age of Enlightenment to the laser displays of recent times. Since illumination is synonymous with the unveiling of a 'scene', with revelation of a transparency without which appearances would be nothing, only a narrow conception could still talk of light simply in terms of the lighting of places. For how can one fail to see, behind those dazzling electro-optical displays, that the public image is on the way to replacing public space, and that the political stage will not be able to do without indirect lighting, any more than it has been able to do without direct artificial lighting? With its origins in the city-theatre organized around the public spectacle of agora, forum or parvis, then in the *cinecittà* of Western modernity, the contemporary *'telecittà'* today establishes the *commutation of perceptible appearances* through the feats of satellites, Hertzian networks and optical fibre cables. In its respective time, each of these 'urban representations' has known how to use the spectacle of transparency, of public illumination, to develop its culture and collective imagination.

* * *

An exceptional situation may serve to illustrate this point. In the spring of 1989, between May and June, Beijing students decided to demonstrate for 'democracy'. They gathered and gradually took over Tiananmen Square, not setting any time limit to their occupation – an old practice which goes back, not to the sit-ins of the sixties (as some have suggested), but to the Greek City where the public space of the agora was the guarantee of the citizens' political unity against the threat of a tyrant.

At the time of Gorbachev's arrival on 14 May, they numbered three hundred thousand, and three days later a million. Profiting from the fact that most of the international agencies had sent their cameras and reporters, and even such top editorial writers as Dan Rather, to cover the reconciliation of the two Communist giants, the Chinese students demanded live coverage of the Tiananmen events so that pictures of the country's most famous public square should be broadcast not only to the world but, above all, to Shanghai, Canton and everywhere else in China.

This demand was rejected by the authorities, and the eventual introduction of martial law was accompanied by a massacre of the population of Beijing by the tanks of the People's Liberation Army. What had already happened in Czechoslovakia after the Prague Spring, or in Poland with the decree establishing an 'internal state of war', was now being reproduced in Asia. The people's army was crushing the people.

But let us return to the 'illumination' of these events by the world's press agencies. Aware that the presence of fifteen hundred journalists in Beijing was of extreme political importance, the students repeatedly showed signs of collusion with their far-off TV 'viewers' by writing banners in French or English, by deploying exotic symbols such as the 'statue of liberty' beneath the portrait of Mao Tse-tung, or by making frequent references to the French Revolution. Formerly, the surface of the agora or the parade ground of a garrison town corresponded to the 'surface area' of the men under arms: citizen-soldiers in Ancient democracy or enlisted troops of fortified towns. 'March separately, strike together': this infantry maxim also fitted the gathering of citizens on the public square; the adjoining streets enabled them to fly to where the public power was identified with the crowd united in the face of external aggression or civil war.

Curiously enough, with the public image of Tiananmen Square broadcast all over the world, we saw both an infinite extension of that surface area (thanks to the real-time interface of the television screen) and a miniaturization of it in the shape of a 51 cm cathode screen that did not seriously convey any depth of field. Hence the importance of the fact that in Hong Kong during that crucial period, not only private television but *the giant screen in the city stadium* was used to unite people collectively with what was taking place at the heart of the Chinese capital.

This was a kind of 'teletopia'[6] in which real-time continuity made up for the absence of real-space contiguity. For a time, the stadium and giant screen in Hong Kong became inseparable from Tiananmen Square, as the square already was from millions of television viewers around the world. However much the forbidden city may ban it, things at one end of the earth are made visible, accessible, at the other end, thanks to the energy of a *living light*, at once electro-optical and acoustic, whose effects on society will be incomparably more important than those of electrification were more than half a century ago.

Real time, delayed time, two times, two 'movements'. On 15 May 1989, the students gathered on Tiananmen Square demanded *live* news coverage – a fruitless effort on their part.

After the tragic events of 7 June in Beijing, Chinese television constantly broadcast *recorded* material, shot by automatic police surveillance cameras, of certain excesses against isolated vehicles and soldiers – always without showing the peaceful occupation of the square or the massacre of its occupants by the People's Republic of China. The choice of image or, to be more precise, the *time* of the image chosen determined China's current political reality – as if, in the end, the country's vast expanse and the huge numbers living in it counted for less than the instant in time chosen to speak of it, to show what was really happening there; as if the real time and real space of the Tiananmen events disturbed the Chinese leaders so much that they had to temper its effects through a *replay*.

It is a strange politics when public images shown with calculated delay are supposed to staunch the disastrous consequences, as the ramparts of the public space and the laws of the city used to block the threat of subversion or aggression. Not only is the day and hour of *concrete* action chosen as before; now there is a decision to obscure the immediate event *temporally and temporarily*, while the actors, the students on Tiananmen Square, are subjected to physical repression.

The events may well be described as a 'siege', a new kind of 'state of siege': not so much an army encirclement of city-space as a *temporal siege*, a siege of the real time of public information. The key element is no longer the familiar censorship preventing disclosure of things that the state wishes to keep secret; it is *the replaying of recorded material*, the retarded ignition of the living light of events.

This 'war over real time' finally shows how right Louis-Ferdinand Céline was at the end of his life, when he said in disillusion: 'For the moment only the facts count, and not even they for very long.'

That moment has now passed, in China as in the wider world: what is done can be undone by means of interactive telecommunications; a 'teletopian' reality has the upper hand over the topical reality of the event. On 9 June 1989, Chinese television solemnly announced that the Army would fire without warning upon anyone carrying a camera or other photographic device.

* * *

The mutation currently under way is confirmed by another, final aspect: namely the crisis of the household car or, more precisely, its symbolic decline to the advantage of other objects, more eccentric vehicles. 'The car will be the last of your worries' – a slogan placed above the Ford stand at the Paris motor show in 1988 – was a wonderful illustration of this process. For it is a decline which, as always, adorns itself with a maximum of useless accessories, rather as the event itself changed its name to the 'World Motor Show'.

In fact, what is really global today is live television; a particular car, whether for sport or transport, is never more than a local object. This explains the recent success of the all-weather vehicle, the famous 4 × 4 which tries to escape the rut of the beaten track. It is an eccentric trial indeed – an attempt to leave the way, the motorway, at any cost.

As we have seen, the image is now the only high-performance vehicle, the real-time image which is supplanting the space where the car still moves from one place to another. In the end, the crisis of the household car is rather like the crisis of the neighbourhood cinema. How many of those dark halls found themselves turned into garages or service-stations, before these in turn became supermarkets or, more recently still, recording studios or newspaper headquarters!

As Fellini put it a short time ago: 'I no longer travel, I only have fits of moving around.' For as fever or energy occupies and possesses us, we no longer dwell in the motive energy of any 'means of transport' – hence the major risk posed by the various 'speed' drugs.

The cinema, Alfred Hitchcock used to say, is armchairs with people inside. Even if the saloon-car bucket seats are for the moment less empty than the cinema armchairs, we should not have any illusions. How much longer will we accept the tedium of the motorway journey?

In Japan television has already invaded taxis and high-rise lifts. Just as dogs are banned from garden squares, cars no longer enter pedestrian zones in some central areas; they go into exile on Paris's ring boulevard while awaiting completion of the super-ring boulevard, or the ultra-rapid underground laser system in which cars will think they are the Metro.

How to make a journey without actually moving from one place to another? How to vibrate in unison? These questions should soon lead to different means of transport and transmission, quite unrelated to the domestic contraption that still serves us today.

Let us look more closely. We no longer turn a switch on our radio or television set; we touch a control or press a key on our remote-control pad. Even our quartz watches have a digital display instead of hands that move around.

'This will replace that,' wrote old Victor Hugo referring to book and cathedral. Will it not be the same tomorrow with screen and limousine? Until when will we *really* keep moving from place to place?

Was it not again the Japanese who recently invented the *bo-do-kahn*, a vibrating pillow that allows you to listen rhythmically to a walkman? Even the rising sun no longer casts its moving rays upon Japanese apartments bathed in sunlight by optical fibre.

Moreover, the people in charge tell us that in the Osaka conurbation, with a population of twenty million, cable networks are already being implanted beneath the motorways so that images can travel through the cars' subsoil. Listen to the Formula One world champion Alain Prost: 'Real speed is to approach obstacles with the impression that you are moving in a slow-motion film.' And the former rally-driver Bernard Darniche stated soon after retiring from competition: 'For me, the ideal car is a mobile video-control.'

Why try to hide it? The only way of saving the private car is to fit it with a temporal video-image compressor: a *turbo-compressor of the real-time image*.

The talking car that warns drivers of engine trouble is a mistake, once *road simulators* for motoring schools are on sale for a hundred thousand francs (the price of a new vehicle). What is needed is a car that actually sees other vehicles *over the horizon*, so that car speed and audiovisual speed are rendered compatible. Maybe the Prometheus project that unites twelve European companies within the framework of Eureka is actually working on such an idea. After all, the 'travel pilot' devised by the Blaupunkt corporation is already just an obsolete guidance system, given that electronic chips of less than one micron will soon each contain the equivalent of the whole US road network.

At a time when a single videodisc can depict all the different journeys in a town – Aspen, Colorado, as it happens – how can there not be attempts to give motoring a new 'perspective' in which the temporal depth of the electronic image prevails over the spatial depth of the motorway network?

Recent advertising for the Thomson washing-machine described this household object as a 'washing-computer'. So how can one fail to grasp that tomorrow's transport machine will first of all be a 'driving-computer', in which the audiovisual feats of the electronic dashboard will prevail over the optical qualities of the field beyond the windscreen?

Just as parachute exercises are moving more and more in the direction of 'relative flight', so will car travel develop from a means of

absolute physical transport to a means of 'relative transport' associated with instantaneous transmission, the kinematic energy of the
video-computer image advantageously replacing the kinetic energy
of engine capacity.

As higher speeds progressively disentitle all others, the TGV and
the ultrasonic aeroplane will not change anything. The *time-reducing
machine* is no longer the motor-car but audiovisual and real-time
technologies.

A few years ago, the Cartier Foundation for Contemporary Art
exhibited a superb collection of Ferraris, a veritable symposium of
coupés, saloons and convertibles. But this luxury display in the Jouy-
en-Josas park merely illustrated the evolution of 'aerodynamics', a
science as antiquated in the age of computer-assisted design and
driving as the aesthetics of old antique furniture has long since been.

Notes

1. Symbolically enough, this electronic surveillance system is operated from the
basements of the Paris City Hall.

2. See Jules Romain, *La Vision extra-rétinienne et le sens paroptique*, Paris: Gallimard, 1964.

3. See Gilles Cohen-Tannoudji and Michel Spiro, *La Matière-espace-temps*, Paris:
Fayard, 1986.

4. A harbinger of such eccentricity appeared in the thirties with the sudden surge
of aerial advertising. 'Skywriting' was then quite a common practice.

5. On 19 October 1987, the computerized Wall Street crash gave us a preview of
the negative effects of that instantaneous link-up of financial markets which is commonly known as the Big Bang.

6. See in this connection the plan for 'decentralization of the capital of Europe'
which I submitted to the Élysée Palace on 14 July 1988.

2

THE LAST VEHICLE

Tomorrow, to learn space will be as useful as learning to drive a car.

Werner von Braun

In Tokyo you can see a new swimming-pool with a strong-current area where swimmers remain *stationary*. A brisk stretch of water prevents you from advancing, so that you have to exert the power of movement to remain where you are. In the manner of a home trainer or a moving walkway used in the wrong direction, the dynamic waters have no other purpose than to get competitive swimmers to fight the energy crossing space to meet them, energy which takes on the dimensions of the Olympic pool, as the rollers of a home trainer replace the velodrome.

Whoever exercises here, then, becomes less a moving body than an island, a *pole of inertia*. As on stage, everything is concentrated on the spot, everything is played out in the privileged instant of an act, the immeasurable instant that replaces extension and protracted periods of time. No longer a golf course but a 'video performance', no longer a road circuit but a track simulator: *space no longer stretches out ahead; the moment of inertia replaces constant movement*.

A similar tendency may be observed in museum design. The largest exhibition areas have recently become *temporal cubbyholes* inversely proportional to their general dimension: *twice the space to cover, twice less time to spend*. The visit speeds up according to the length of the picture line. With too much space and not enough time, the museum bathes in useless expanses which the exhibits no longer manage to furnish – probably because they still try to spread into those distant surfaces now devoid of attraction, after the fashion of the grand perspectives of the classical age.

Attentive visitors used to spend a long time considering the major works in whose memory our monumental buildings were erected.

But now it is 'amateurs' who shoot through them, a public that should be held fast for more than one instant yet races all the faster as the space at its disposal becomes more voluminous.

Monuments of a time when artistic works are eclipsed rather than exhibited, contemporary museums vainly try to assemble and put on view objects that are normally kept out of the way in workshop-studios, in laboratories of a deeper perception which the 'passing visitor', distracted by his or her animating tension, will never actually experience. In this same perspective of 'holding back', of restricting the 'time of passage', let us note another manifesto-type project, namely the reconstruction of the State of Israel in miniature, where, to quote the official proposal, 'visitors would be able to admire, *in complete safety and with a minimum of travel*, a faithful copy of the Holocaust Museum, a piece of the Wailing Wall, and a scaled-down Sea of Galilee with a few cubic metres of original water' – to which the directors of the foundation created for this purpose would like to add a display of materials and electronic components produced by Israeli industry. This demonstration of extra-territoriality would take place off Douarnenez on Tristan Island, which would have been ceded by France to the Israeli State.

Even if this utopia never comes about, it perfectly expresses the *telluric contraction*, the sudden 'overexposure' which today affects the size of a territory, the surface area of the largest objects, as well as the very nature of our travels. It is travelling on the spot, with an inertia that is to the passing landscape what the 'freeze-frame' is to the film. And it is the coming of a last generation of remote communication vehicles, with no possible comparison to those of the transport revolution – as if the conquest of space proved in the end to be only of *images of space*. For if the end of the nineteenth century and the beginning of the twentieth saw the arrival of the dynamic automotive vehicle – on railway and road and then in the air – it seems that the end of this century heralds a final shift with the advent of the static *audiovisual vehicle*, a substitute for bodily movement and an extension of domestic inertia which will mark the definitive triumph of sedentariness.

The transparency of space as the horizon of our travels or journeys is thus being supplanted by a *cathodic transparency* that consummates the invention of glass four thousand years ago and plate glass two thousand years ago, as well as of that enigmatic shop 'window' which has so marked urban architecture from the Middle Ages down to our own times or, rather, until the recent development of the *electronic window* (most accomplished in the 'flight simulator') as the last horizon of our journeys.

Abundant proof is offered by the recent evolution of amusement parks into laboratories of *physical sensations* complete with toboggans, catapults and centrifuges, reference models for the training of aviators and cosmonauts. According to those responsible for this, the fun of the fair is also heading towards collective experimentation with purely *imaginary* mental sensations.

Having been, in the last century, a theatre of lost bodily sensations for a working-class population deprived of enriching and varied physical activities, the leisure park is on the point of becoming a stage for pure optical illusions, a generalization of the non-place of simulation with its fictitious journeys offering everyone electronic hallucination or intoxication – a 'loss of sight' replacing the nineteenth-century loss of physical activity. It is true, however, that, in parallel with the fairground occupations of acrobat and trapeze artist, the 'panoramas', 'dioramas' and other forms of cinematography paved the way for the *'panrama'* or *'Géode'*, a hemispheric cinema prefigured by Grimoin-Sanson's *'cinerama ballon'*. In fact, these may be seen as primitive forms of our present-day *audiovisual vehicles*; the American Hale's Tours made the project clear enough, some of the 'tours' between 1898 and 1908 actually being financed by railroad companies. Let us recall that those films shot from the front of a locomotive or the panoramic platform at the rear of a train were then shown to the public in halls exactly resembling the railway coaches of the time. Some of these short films were made by Billy Bitzer, later to be D.W. Griffith's chief cameraman.

At this point, however, we should go back to the sources of the illusion of motion, to the Lumière Brothers' *Arrival of a Train at La Ciotat Station* (1895), and above all to Eugène Promio's invention of the very first tracking shot in the spring of 1896. Listen to what he says about it.

> It was in Italy that I first had the idea of panning shots. In Venice, on a boat along the Grand Canal from the station to my hotel, I watched the banks shoot past and thought that *if motionless cinema makes it possible to reproduce moving objects, the reverse might also be attempted by reproducing motionless objects with the aid of moving cinema.* I then made a film and sent it to Lyons with a request that Louis Lumière tell me what he thought of it. His response was favourable.

To grasp the importance of this inauguration of 'moving cinema' – or, in other words, of the first *static vehicle* – we need to take another look back. Without going as far as Nadar's 'aerostatic pictures'

(1858) that were the origin of filmic weightlessness, let us note that it was only in 1910 that the first 'aeronautical shots' were taken, on board a Farman aircraft. As to the rail-mounted 'dolly' that is an inseparable part of contemporary cinema, it first appeared four years later during the shooting of *Cabiria* by Giovanni Pastrone. We should also mention the Agit Prop trains of the 1918–25 period and Dziga Vertov's use of railway images flashing past. It was in the spring of 1918 that Vertov joined the 'Current Events Cinema Committee' in Moscow, but he waited until 1923 before helping to set up a 'Cinema Automobile Department' for emergency use in covering important events – a kind of forerunner of television 'video broadcasting'. This new vehicle, at once automotive and audiovisual, finally changed our perception of the world: *optics and kinematics merged together*. Einstein's point of view theory, later called the 'special theory of relativity', saw the light of day in 1905, and ten years later it was followed by the general theory of relativity. As an aid to understanding, both often resorted to the metaphor of the train, tram or lift, vehicles of a physical theory which owes them almost everything, since, as we shall see, the transport revolution of the same period involved a characteristic change in the phenomenon of *arrival* with the gradual negation of the time interval and the accelerated retention of the time between departure and arrival. Spatial distance suddenly gave way to temporal distance alone, the most distant journeys being hardly anything more than interludes.

As we have already noted, however, although the nineteenth century and much of the twentieth did witness the rise of the automotive vehicle in all its forms, the *vehicle mutation is far from over*. For it will lead, as before only faster, from unbridled nomadism to the definitive inertia or sedentariness of whole societies.

Contrary to appearances, it is the audiovisual vehicle which has been thrusting itself forward since the thirties – radio, television, radar, sonar and the nascent electronic optics, first in the war and then, despite the massive development of the private car, in the 'nuclear peace' that has seen the *computer revolution* indispensable for the running of the various policies of military and economic deterrence. Since the 1960s, then, the key arena has no longer been the communication routes of a given geographical territory (hence the lifting of price controls and other regulation of public transport) but the electronic ether of telecommunications.

Now everything arrives without any need to depart. The special arrival of dynamic vehicles, moving and then self-moving, has suddenly been replaced by the general arrival of images and sounds in the static vehicles of the audiovisual. Polar inertia is setting in. The instant interface is being substituted for the longest journey times. After *distance/time* took over from space in the nineteenth century, it is now the *distance/speed* of electronic imagery which is the coming thing. *The picture freeze is replacing non-stop parking.*

* * *

According to Ernst Mach, the whole universe is mysteriously present in each place and at each instant. And indeed, if each moving (or self-moving) vehicle conveys a specific vision, a perception of the world that is but the artefact of its speed of movement within its surroundings on land, sea or air, then conversely each of the optical or sound images of the perceived world represents a 'vehicle' or vector of communication inseparable from its speed of transmission. This has been the case since the instantaneous correction of the image in the *passive optics* of Galileo's telescope lens, right down to our modern 'means of telecommunication' with their *active optics* of video computing.

It is no longer possible, then, to distinguish the dynamic vehicle from the static vehicle, the automotive from the audiovisual. (The recent *primacy of arrival* over departure, over all departures and therefore all journeys and trajectories, accomplishes a mysterious exorcism.) We are faced with an inertia of the moment, of each place and instant of the present world – an inertia which ultimately resembles the principle of non-separability, the principle of an inertia which completes the principle of quantum indeterminacy.

Even if we are today witnessing attempts at a technological mixing of the two vehicles – for example, the systematic use in Japan of video landscapes in high-rise lifts – and even if long-haul aircraft now regularly show feature movies, this momentary conjunction will in the end inevitably lead to elimination of the slower vector. The *fuite en avant* of the high-speed train and the supersonic aeroplane, together with the deregulation affecting them both, indicate better than any prediction that it is the vehicle or vector of terrestrial, maritime and aerial automotivity which is really under threat.

The *era of intensive time* does not belong to physical means of transport. Unlike the past era of extensive time, it belongs entirely to the means of telecommunication: that is, it is an era of *staying on the spot*, of *housebound inertia*.

This is demonstrated by the recent evolution of the motor car, and of Formula One racing. For their inability seriously to match the feats of the audiovisual results in constant changes to racing car performance, competition rules, vehicle weight, petrol reserves, and sometimes (the last straw!) even horsepower.

But the dynamic land vehicle most symptomatic of this sporting involution is the dragster (and the hot rod), whose motto might be: 'How to go nowhere, or anyway less and less far (400 metres, 200) but faster and faster?'

This intensive competition perhaps tends, at the extreme, to make finishing line and starting line coincide – a feat similar to that achieved by the *live* televised interface. Nor is the evolution of the domestic car any different, since there is now a kind of *automobile self-sufficiency* which makes it more and more like a detached piece of furniture. This accounts for the relocation or duplication of accessories, personal items, stereo systems, radio-telephones, telex, video equipment, so that the means of transport *over distance* imperceptibly becomes a means of transport *on the spot*, a vehicle for the transporting of merriment, music, speed . . .

In fact, if all automotive vehicles – terrestrial, marine and aerial – are now less 'mounts' in the equestrian sense than mounts in the optician's sense of *frames*, it is because the self-propelling vehicle is becoming less a vector of physical movement than a means of representation, *the support for a more or less high-speed optics of the surrounding space.*

The more or less distant vision that comes with travelling is gradually giving way to a more or less high-speed 'prevision' of arrival at destination, a generalized arrival of images and information which now takes the place of our continual movement from place to place.

This explains that secret correspondence between the static architecture of buildings and the media inertia of the audiovisual vehicle which establishes itself with the emergence of the *intelligent home*, or rather of the smart interactive city where *teleport* succeeds sea port, railway station and international airport.

A famous actress once fended off an indiscreet journalist by answering: 'I live everywhere!' Tomorrow, with the aesthetics or logic of the disappearance of architectonics, we can be sure that *we will all live everywhere*, like those 'video zoo' animals present only in their picture on a screen, filmed somewhere or other, yesterday or the day before, in some place of no consequence. In those sprawling suburbs of filmic unreality, *audiovisual speed* will at last be for our interior domestic architecture what *automotive speed* was already for the architecture of the city, for the whole layout of the region.

'Ground simulators' will then take over from flight simulators. Shut up in our *cathode display cases*, we shall become the tele-actors in a living cinema already signalled by those 'son et lumière' displays which everyone, from André Malraux through Jack Lang to Léotard, has defended on the pretext that they safeguard our heritage in real estate.

To become a film therefore seems to be our common destiny. And it seems so all the more since Philippe de Villiers, the man in charge of the Puy-du-Fou 'Cinéscénie' in the Vendée and more recently secretary of state for culture and communication, got the idea of promoting 'scenic trips in heritage sites' more or less everywhere, in order to make France's historical monuments more appealing and thus more competitive with the imported Disneyland near Paris or the 'World of Adventures' near London.

After the theatrical setting of the agora, forum and parvis that traditionally accompanied the history of cities, we now have *cinematic settings* of one commune, region or heritage site after another, their active population transformed for a while into extras in a history that it is thought fitting to revive – whether it is the Vendée war starring Philippe de Villiers, or the centuries-long merits of the city of Lyons, starring Jean-Michel Jarre. It is true, however, that the present minister of culture himself sacrificed to the same phenomenon when he inaugurated a more sophisticated audiovisual practice under the 'Salamander' programme by funding an interactive videodisc visit of the castles of the Loire. In this 'son et lumière' at home, those who used to visit the tourist past will become *video visitors*, 'tele-lovers of old stones', with discs of Cheverny and Chambord alongside Mozart and Verdi in their collection.

* * *

'You no longer dream, you are dreamt, silence' – wrote Henri Michaux in his poem 'La Ralentie'. The inversion begins. The film is run through again in reverse. The water flows back up the bottle. We walk backwards, but faster and faster. The involution leading to inertia speeds up. Even our desire freezes in a media detachment that is ever more pronounced. After the display-window prostitutes of Amsterdam, the fifties striptease and the sixties peep-shows, the time has come for video pornography.

In Rue Saint-Denis in Paris, the list of deadly sins comes down to the new technologies of the image: BETACAM, VHS, VIDEO 2000, and so on, while awaiting erotic robotics, the vision machine, and so on.

This is also how things are in the field of military conflict. After the home trainer used by First World War aviators, the revolving arm-chair for pilot training in the Second, and the centrifuge for future astronauts at NASA (a life-size test of people's ability to cope with weightlessness), the last ten years have seen the development of more and more efficient 'simulators' for would-be enthusiasts of supersonic flight. The most perfect of these devices, a one-person projection dome eight metres in diameter, will soon present a constant image in a field of vision close to 300 degrees, the pilot's helmet being fitted with an eye-tracked optical system. To heighten the realism still further, the trainee will wear an inflatable flying suit that simulates the effects of gravitational pressure associated with acceleration.

But the really key piece, already being tested, is a simulation system derived from the oculometer. Finally free of the screen, *images of aerial combat will thus be directly projected in the pilot's eyeballs*, thanks to a helmet fitted with optical fibres. This hallucinatory training device, whose effects resemble those of drugs, signals a tendency for any stage or screen to disappear in favour of the 'seat', but it will be a trap seat [*siège/piège*] where *perception is programmed in advance according to the calculating power of the computer's inference motor*.

Faced with this static vehicle of the future, I think the very concepts of energy and motor need to be reconsidered. For if physicists still distinguish two kinds of energy – potential energy and the kinetic energy that causes movement – perhaps we should now, ninety years after the invention of the cinema travelling shot, add a third form, namely the *kinematic energy* which results from the effect of movement and its greater or lesser speed upon ocular, optical and opto-electronic perception.

In this sense, the new *simulation industry* would appear as the application of this last energy resource. The calculating power of the latest generation of computers makes them somehow resemble a final type of motor, the *kinematic motor*.

But we would be missing the essential point if we did not touch again on that primacy of space over time which is today expressed in the primacy of (instantaneous) arrival over departure. If *time depth* now prevails over field depth, it is because our old schemes of temporality have undergone significant mutation. Here as elsewhere, in our ordinary everyday life, *we are passing from the extensive time of history to the intensive time of an instantaneity without history* made possible by the technologies of the hour. Automotive, audiovisual and computer technologies are all moving towards the same restriction or contraction of time. And the telluric contraction calls into question not only the surface area of territories but also the architecture of buildings and apartments.

If time is history, speed is only a perspectival hallucination that is the ruin of all territory, all chronology. It is a spatio-temporal hallucination obviously resulting from intensive exploitation of *kinematic energy* whose motor is today the audiovisual vehicle, as the moving then automotive vehicle was yesterday for kinetic energy, synthetic images finally replacing the energies of the same name invented in the last century.

We should therefore no longer trust the third dimension as the measure of size; *relief is no longer reality.* For now reality is hidden in the flatness of televisual images and representations – hence the return to the block under siege and the corpse-like fixity of an interactive, cockpit-like abode, where the main piece of furniture is the *seat*, the ergonomic chair of the physically handicapped, and – who knows? – the *bed*, a sofa-bed for crippled viewers, a divan on which to be dreamt without dreaming, a bench seat on which to be moved along without moving . . .

Strangely enough, with this recent invention of a vehicle for movement without moving, we are back again with the early days of the car – as if growing inertia returned everything to its point of departure, to this seat as the reference model of nascent automotivity.

In fact, as a domestic automat applied to physical movement, the private car was originally part of the furniture boom. In a line descending from the old sedan chair and the Asian palanquin or rickshaw, from the rocking chair, swivel chair and the first *wheelchair* (invented by Jacob for Louis XVIII in 1820), the motor car actually appeared as the inheritor of the *seat that rests the lower limbs*.[1] The technical affinities of the automobile are thus not mainly with the chariot, mail coach or other kinds of diligence; the comfort of the motor vehicle makes it more like a *moving piece of furniture*. Indeed, the extreme fragility of the early Ford or Daimler-Benz prototypes cannot but call to mind a baby carriage, if not a prosthesis for the physically disabled.

Today, in a world of porn-video booths, video-artists' installations, driving simulators and various 'datalands' of computer graphics, the spread of audiovisual technologies and consoles takes us back to the seat as *a post from which to control the near or far environment*, as it is offered to customers by the manufacturers of orthopaedic equipment. Even the latest supersonic fighter aircraft are designed around the cockpit – or, in other words, around the instrument panel and ejector seat of the 'elite pilot' who has become the perfect example of the disabled person, his very survival depending upon the motor and audiovisual feats of his equipment. *The equipped invalid is thus paradoxically on a par with the overequipped able person.*

So we wait for this 'blind cockpit' to perfect its synthesis of the real and the simulated, in which a dynamic vehicle (a state-of-the-art flying machine) is associated with an ultra-sophisticated audiovisual static vehicle, thanks to the first *onboard ground simulator* that will give the pilot indirect and constantly updated vision of the landscape and weather conditions of the region he is overflying. Loss of ocular perception will thus enable future war pilots to fly in broad daylight when it is really night, or to fly in clear weather below the range of enemy radar amid the wintriest of fogs. The remote-control video panel is thus clearly the origin of the last vehicle, the audiovisual vehicle that will revolutionize our relationship to the environment as the automotive vehicle once transformed the real geography of town and country.

Curiously, the convergence of cinema and aeronautics – both born at the same time, moreover – keeps driving forward the technology of representation and communication, with today's unification of computer video with astronautics and the boom in communication satellites that are also means of instant tele-representation of the present world. It is as if the *filmic weightlessness* of the sequence of frames and then video images tended to merge with that of the overflight by (spatial or aerial) machines, definitively uniting *the vehicle of the image* with *the image of the flying vehicle*. This unity of optics and kinematics requires that the vector of physical movement (the means of transport over distance) should no longer be separated from its specific vision – confirmation, if any were needed, that kinematic energy, the last unexploited form, has finally arrived.

Let us note here that the attraction which animal and human flight held for many European and American photographers in the nineteenth century – among others, Nadar and his friend Marey, the inventor of chronophotography in 1882 – was linked to the hope of achieving 'aerial views', that is, of *acquiring the special vision of an aerial means of transport*.

Those who wanted to fly in those days mainly wanted to 'go in the air' and not 'to go somewhere', as was later the case with commercial aviation. For the famous 'conquest of the air' was the conquest of an *incomparable spectacle*, of an omnipresence analogous to that of the divine gaze.

Nor should we forget that in 1884 Étienne-Jules Marey was titular president of the French Société de Navigation Aeriénne, and that at the instigation of Samuel Langley, the American aeronaut, his research on liquid flows and wind tunnels was being subsidized by the Smithsonian Institution. This was the same Langley who later gave his name to the research centre where a supersonic wind tunnel capable of reaching Mach 16 was built in the 1950s – a tunnel where, this time, most of the engines necessary for the 'conquest of space' were developed.

Today the work of Graeme Ferguson, inventor of the IMAX/OMNIMAX system and director of the hemispheric film *The Dream Is Alive*, is jointly funded by NASA and the same Smithsonian Institution that once subsidized the pioneer of chronophotography.

Finally, disputes over the origins of the cinema (often scandalously attributed to the Lumière Brothers alone) have helped to conceal, and then to conjure away altogether, this relationship between the invention of cinema and of aviation. Yet there is an instructive coincidence between the *parade of cinema sequences*, the filmic weightlessness of the frame, and the invention of an aerial *kinematic parade*. The latter is the start of a real weightlessness this time, demonstrated by man's flight on board a *motor-driven* craft that makes it possible for him to modify at will the shooting of aerial sequences.

It was necessary to wait until 1914–18 before the necessities of strategic observation again united what had been so wrongly separated in a vain dispute over academic precedence: that is, the film *camera* and its kinematic vessel, the *aircraft*. This amalgam of aeronautic vehicle and onboard camera achieves a model of *panoramic apperception*, the first intensive use of a new energy whose future development will be assured by television and then telematics, up to the instant orbital perception that we know today. In 1933, indeed, Vladimir Zworykin presented his newly invented 'iconoscope' (an early name for the electronic television) not as a means of mass communication, but as a way of increasing the range of human vision. He even had the idea of installing a camera on a rocket so as to observe the universe.

Disillusioned and impotent at the end of his life, the former observation pilot from the Great War, the film-maker Jean Renoir, said to his secretary: 'Give my wheelchair a push. I'm like a camera that's just ticking over.'

* * *

In the end, each advance in transport is hardly any more than a freeing of the seat for further rapid development. Let us recall the birth of the home trainer, that equivalent of the knight's old 'wooden horse' where one learnt piloting on an articulated frame that simulated the movements of a biplane. After 1914, when better aircraft performance compelled an improvement in aviators' reflexes, the first scientific experiments were conducted into the state of weightlessness.

In June 1918 Doctor Garsaux, then the only doctor attached to the aeronautics technical department, was appointed at Louis Bleriot's request to determine the acceleration limit that a human being could tolerate. The cardiologists declared themselves incompetent to judge. The director of the School of Mining Engineering replied that no restrictions were planned with regard to the acceleration of lift-cages, for example. Professor Broca agreed to centrifuge some dogs that would be obtained by Professor Lapicque. Here there is a nice titbit concerning the discovery of the centrifuge: 'With our thoughts on a revolving platform in Luna Park called the 'buttery plate', which measured six metres in diameter, we went to acquire it for ourselves. But it had just been bought by the District Engineers!' explains Doctor Garsaux. The first animals were therefore dealt with in a centrifugal dryer from a gunpowder factory, 1.50 metres in diameter. It was possible to conclude, however, that the dogs could tolerate 30g and succumbed only between 84g and 97g, according to their position vis-à-vis the rotation axis.[2]

In this original account we find the experimental vocation of the 'fairground trades', with the perfecting of the swivel seat, the *gyrating chair* and the *centrifuge* as models of mechanical simulators for the newly developing aviation sector, and soon for the study of supersonic and extra-atmospheric vessels.

This research was subsequently conducted in Holland by Jongbloed and Noyons, in Germany by Koenel, Ranke and Diringshofen, and in the United States by Armstrong and Heim, where it eventually focused on the physiological problems of breaking various acceleration limits, the sound barrier, the heat barrier, and so on.

In 1957 the most powerful and modern centrifuge, built by the Navy, was to be found in Johnsville, Pennsylvania. The exercise gondola was mounted on a 15 m arm to which the engine could give almost immediate acceleration of 0 to 75 m/s.

In addition, the gondola could be bent at almost any angle, and a cam-set inserted in the position command made it possible to make the gondola jump weakly or strongly, slow or fast, imitating the movements of an airplane accelerating out of control. [. . .] To begin with, *the engineers mounted a complete X-15 cockpit in the gondola*, then they had the idea of linking the centrifuge to an electric commutator that would transcribe the dial readings from the central pivot onto the instrument panel displays. This made it possible to 'pilot the airplane', not only according to what the instruments said, but also taking into account *a whole theoretical range of acceleration* [. . .]. When the acceleration neared the maximum that the device could stand – a value of 9 or even 10g – I fainted with my head drooping on my side, my eyes turned up, my facial skin grotesquely deformed. *All the trials were filmed by an automatic camera inside the gondola.*[3]

From the Venetian gondola of Eugène Promio, that original enthusiast of 'mobile cinema', to the US Navy centrifuge sixty years later (where the tracking shot no longer has canal banks rushing past but, instead, the wrinkles of a disfigured face), the vessel and its vision have undergone considerable transformation. Alongside the particle accelerator that makes the ultimate components of matter appear on a screen, the centrifuge represents a similar effort – to make the outer limits of consciousness, up to the point of fainting, appear on the passenger's features.

Long before this kind of one-man cyclotron, however, Colonel J.P. Stapp (a medical specialist in the effects of high-altitude ejection at supersonic speeds) installed at Edwards Base in the Mojave Desert a rail sledge driven by a set of rockets which imparted a terrifying initial acceleration: *1600 metres in a few seconds at more than 1000 km/h*. After its arrival – if that is the right word – the jet-propelled sledge plunged into water and underwent an equally devastating deceleration. All this to test the *ejection seats* of the future!

As we can see, then, *the vehicle for going at speed* (that is, *for going nowhere*) has numerous precursors in the fairgrounds and amusement parks and the training camps for aeronautical or astronautical levitation. Thus, along with the present-day 'hot rodders', Colonel Stapp – a real experimenter with machines to test man's limits and especially the features of ejected flyers – is a necessary character in this second 'transport revolution' which is taking us from the age of the dynamic automotive vehicle to the age of the static audiovisual vehicle. In the space park at Huntsville, Alabama, simulators of theoretical behaviour have now supplanted those instruments of torture thought fit for interrogation in the Middle Ages.

From the circular accelerator for aeronauts described by Doctor Garsaux, through Doctor Stapp's linear accelerator, to NASA's giant centrifuge preparing astronauts to conquer the Moon fifty years later, research into the effects of theoretical acceleration has never ceased to advance and to revolutionize the nature of both vehicles and fixtures. Rocking seat and swivel seat lead via the gyrating chair to the centrifuge of aeronauts and then cosmonauts, while the Bath chair leads to the domestic automotivity of the private car ... the ejector seat of supersonic aircraft and, finally, the high *kinetic* energy-absorbing seat for forced helicopter landings. All these mutations of an ever more autonomous piece of furniture are now culminating, before the computer graphics consoles, in the high *kinematic* energy-absorbing 'graviseat' of flight simulators. To make the scenes more realistic, these simulators give the test pilot low-grade mechanical movements and reinforced pneumatic effects, by using anti-gravity flying suits to compensate for the fixed projection domes of the aerial combat simulators.

The cinema is first of all chairs with people inside, explained Alfred Hitchcock. And the 'conquest of the air' – contemporary, we should not forget, with the invention of the cinema – was first of all an unprecedented spectacle allowing us to go everywhere thanks to the combination of *air-taking* machines (balloon, aeroplane, rocket) with various *picture-taking* devices (photographic, cinematographic, video and computer). Finally, the 'conquest of outer space' is essentially the conquest of what is left of time, *a televisual instantaneity completely necessary for astronautical ubiquitousness*. For whereas the first winged cine-camera marked the conquest of the third dimension of the world as spectacle, the rise of spacecraft and other means of instant remote transmission achieved the conquest of the fourth dimension and thus perfected the inertia of the commanding point of view.

In this orbital state of siege, the whole planet is placed under close surveillance. It is also temporally circumscribed by the instant inter-action of 'telecommunications', another name for that sudden confusion of near and far, inside and outside, whereby *media non-separability* deeply affects the nature of the building, the figure of inertia and therefore the morphological stability of reality.

Today, when someone from television special effects tells us: 'The more pictures there are to see, the less people look; they are not flies', he is warning us, a little late, about audiovisual excesses and the blindness that can result from them. But he seems to forget that active optics marks us out not to become 'tele-viewers' – that happened some time ago – but *to become a film, a televised broadcast*, or in other words, weightless beings whose destiny to pass through walls is as enigmatic as that of our 'final resting-place', which is another

way of calling that *terminal vessel* meant for a population of definitive parking or absolute sedentariness. This inertial confinement of
place, of all geographical places, will make each of us a *tele-actor*
inhabiting not so much the time of clocks and calendars as that truer-
than-nature 'real time' which instantly exiles us from space – from
the very real space which, not so long ago, separated inside from
outside, centre from periphery, as long time spans made it possible
to distinguish cause from effect. Precisely this is *control of the
environment*.

* * *

Already the alcove, the 'cupboard bed' popular in Britanny and the
Auvergne, portended the Kotobuki Capsule Hotel in Osaka whose
three-square-metre cells do not allow you to stand up yet contain a
built-in television and telephone.

This canning of the night recalled the archetype of the camera
obscura and its pinhole. The architecture suddenly closed around the
dreams, to the point where it matched the confinement of bedding.

Today, the industrialization of telecommunications is resuming
this theme. The final resting-place is shrinking before our eyes to a
blind cockpit for the dreams of a population of sleepwalkers. We can
now see that the tumulus *burial chamber*, with its window open to
the skimming light of the winter solstice, inaugurated the optical
principle of directional lighting that led to the camera obscura of
Renaissance perspectivists and brought about a new representation
of the world that would lead to the passive optics of the lens and,
more recently, to active video-computer optics. Thus, just as the
megalithic tomb was the ancestor of our 'film camera', the architect
Kurokawa's capsule refers us back to the myth of the camera
obscura.

In fact, the image which has long been the design material of the
architectural 'project' is now becoming the actual construction material of the 'finished product', with the quickly recognized and
accepted pre-eminence of the screen interface over the wall surface.

Behind this event, or rather this *ad*vent of a new architectonic
order, one easily glimpses the coming mutations of the window,[4] and,
more fundamentally still, those which will sooner or later affect the
doorway as the obligatory threshold that generated (and still gener-
ates) internal space – or, as we should now say, that programmed the

plan and distribution of the building's volumes. For when one touches the limit or frontier between things, everything immediately dissolves into the utmost confusion, beginning with the clear distinction between inside and outside, and therefore, necessarily, the hitherto essential concepts of *entry* and *exit*. Everything that used to imply the architectural need for a *doorway* – and also, at city level, for a *port* and *airport* – disappears with the emergence of the *teleport*, the national 'conveyance machine' of image and sound, the *architecture of the era of generalized arrival*, as revealing today as the station was in the railway age or the garage in the automobile age.

Thus, at this *fin de siècle* which is ushering in the second ('on the spot') transport revolution, the electronic lighting of cameras and monitors mirrors the effects of the electrification of town and country at the beginning of the century; it opens up the home to a new artificial light, an 'electronic daylight' that supplants electric light as the latter once did the rising of the day.

The properties of active optics (electronics and tomorrow's photonics) mainly serve the function no longer of lighting or dispelling darkness, but rather of *dispelling the obstacle of extension*, the immensity of a given territory. The screen opens out to replace not just the 'window', as the oil lamp and then Edison's electric lamp once did, but even the 'doorway' itself, thereby revolutionizing the nature of the house or apartment.

Significantly, it is just when the ground is being laid for home-based teleworking, when teleconferences are proposed as ways for people to meet one another, that a parallel shift is occurring in penal confinement. In France, for example, television sets were installed in prisoners' cells in 1986, ostensibly to counter the 'separation syndrome' but, above all, to avoid excessive use of psychotropic drugs. Though little analysed, this sudden decision to instal television not just in common areas but in the cells themselves represents a characteristic shift. For since Bentham it has been customary to identify prison with the famous panopticon – that is, with central surveillance whereby prisoners are never out of their warders' field of vision.

From now on, prisoners will in turn be able to survey current events on television – an all too obvious point, unless it is inverted to imply that as soon as viewers switch on, it is they, prisoners or not, who are in *the field of television*, a perceptual field over which they evidently have no power except that of suspending it altogether.

A number of recent investigations conducted by private TV channels confirm this inversion of viewpoint. For here, unlike in public sector television, advertisers need *to know who watches what*, and ordinary survey techniques are too unreliable. In one experiment in Oxford, spy-cameras were installed in a number of people's homes without their knowledge. But since the results were still too imprecise, an 'eye-tracked' system linked to the TV set is now being developed that will record people's viewing practice minute by minute during a particular broadcast.

This electronic house-arrest is a clinical symptom of the inertia that is leading to the reign of the static vehicle. Within this same perspective, let us take an innovation in the State of New York, where electronic *transponders* fitted to the persons of six common-law prisoners confine them in the closed circuits of telesurveillance *within their own apartments*, the police being able to monitor their every movement on a screen. If these new-style 'prisoners without partitions' stray too far from their prison-home,[5] a signal is instantly transmitted to the radio-tracking station that keeps them under constant surveillance. As its promoters explain, this 'field prison' can ease the pressure of overcrowding and hence avert the undesirable privatization of prisons, for the detainees have no prison and their confinement remains public! The band attached to their ankle, as the ball and chain once used to be, means that prisoners can go out to do shopping or for a regular job, so long as they do not leave *an area designated by their judges*.

Here Bentham's panopticon is no longer in the detention centre but in the apartment or city, or even the country at large. (This kind of 'distress beacon', coupled with a few Argos satellites, was actually tested a decade or so ago to track the migration of polar bears in the Far North.) Similarly, in the Chizé Forest in the department of Deux-Sèvres, not far from the Poitou Marshes, a CNRS scientific radio-tracking station constantly observes the daytime and nighttime behaviour of the local fauna.

'Watch and punish' (*"Surveiller et Punir"*), wrote Michel Foucault in a famous book. What punishment is involved in this imaginative expansion of imprisonment, this 'media ghettoization' or 'electronic apartheid'? It certainly does not seem to be limited to the penal and military domains (electronic battlefield receivers); it can also be found in the automated company, long-distance trade-union negotiations,[6] and more generally in the mode of development of 'post-industrial' town planning.

For the changes to customary notions of space and time have extended the principle of relativity to the old concept of *surface area*, so that eventually this is replaced with the much underestimated concept of *interface*. But the interface, by establishing the surface area in its media relationship, makes of that relationship a veritable 'face to face'. Thus every surface, however tiny or however huge, now has objective existence only in and through its relationship to observation, to the viewpoint of one observer or another.

It is not exactly usage, then, which defines space, but rather vision or *insight*.

What was previously a legitimate practice in astronomy or astrophysics, as in microphysics, is also becoming legitimate *here below*. What will happen *once we ourselves have become films, television broadcasts, in the homes of distant interlocutors*?

Where the real time of instant transmission prevails over the real space of a region or country actually travelled through, where therefore *the image takes precedence over the physically present thing or being*, the indirect lighting of the electronic image supplants the direct lighting of electricity. Has it not recently become the case that our light-cities are illuminated less by neon lampposts than by cameras positioned in public places, at junctions and on the big avenues? With the installation of 'optical fibre cables', the automatic camera and its monitor will soon take over from electrification. In order to see, one will no longer be content to dispel the external shadows of night, but will also dispel intervals and distances, *exteriority itself* – hence the unnoticed decline of the threshold 'doorway' that used to give access to internal architecture.

In this same perspective of geophysical retention or premonitory miniaturization, we should also note the 'Biosphere II' project currently under way at the foot of the Santa Catalina mountains in Arizona.[7] Not unlike the Israeli plan for Tristan Island described above, this Edwards Air Force Base project involves setting up by the year 1990 a *microcosm* inhabited by eight people, male and female, who will be confined for two years in airtight conditions matching in all but weightlessness those of a colony on a planet without atmosphere – or those which would prevail on earth after a nuclear catastrophe. This artificial ecosystem, spread over an area of roughly 2500 acres, will include two miniature oceans, a scaled-down tropical forest, a lagoon, several marshes, and a desert. Overshadowing everything, a geodesic dome will contain the housing and equipment of the human 'biospherians', and it is said that solar energy and telecommunications will be the only things coming from the outside to these voluntary exiles from earth.

Several official bodies, including NASA and the Smithsonian Institution in Washington, are participating in this experiment in fixed residence. According to Margaret Augustine, the Canadian architect directing the project: 'Biosphere II will be a tool for studying various methods of environmental control.' In other words, it will be an instrument to analyse conditions of individual confinement perfectly resembling those of the disabled or imprisoned – at the very time when plans are afoot, especially in Europe, to do away with prisons and to treat at home severely disabled paraplegics or tetraplegics.

Monk's House, where Virginia Woolf lived, was for her the 'vessel' of motionless navigation. In the thirties the ferry boat was for Le Corbusier and others the model of a 'unified residence', and soon after the war the cabin of the transatlantic aeroplane became the prototype for household equipment. But now that metaphor is out of date. With the 'on the spot' transport revolution, we see alongside specialized rooms (kitchen, shower-room, study or 'sensory deprivation box' for the less deprived) a control post to manage the inflow of data. The apartment thus acquires an instrument panel of its own, a climatized cabin or image cockpit containing all the controls and remote controls for the bodily organs to steer it on its way.

Notes

1. See Paul Virilio, *L'Horizon négatif*, Paris: Galilée, 1984, p. 41.
2. Marcel Julian, *Gens de l'air*, Paris: Le Livre contemporain, 1959.
3. S. Crossfield and C. Blair, *X.15*, Ed. Arthaud 1960. [Retranslated].
4. See Paul Virilio, 'La troisième fenêtre', *Cahiers du cinéma* No. 322, 1981.
5. The term *décloisonnement* [literally 'departitioning'] is part of the jargon of penal reform.
6. At Citroën in 1982 and Renault in 1986, video was used so that the two sides would not actually have to meet in the course of difficult negotiations.
7. See *Science et vie* No. 831, December 1986.

3

KINEMATIC OPTICS

Today the relativity of the visible has become self-evident.

Paul Klee

Creation and Fall of time, daylight orders and regulates not only the elasticity of the day, week, month and year, but also the relativity which has always accompanied the understanding of time, the time of mystics or politicians whose traces have been preserved by history, philosophy and physics. Finally, the special and general theories of relativity resulted in the crisis of temporal and spatial absolutism, the explosion of an infinity of 'local times' brought on by the constancy of the speed of light – a *speed of light* which now illuminates extension and duration with a new daylight, since it seems agreed that speed causes time to expand at the moment when it shrinks space.

This view of the physical world, which actually resembles a general optics or aesthetics (so much so that Einstein once thought of replacing the term 'relativity theory' with *Standpunktslehre* or 'point of view theory'), concurs with the metaphysical vision of the apostle Peter: 'With the Lord one day is like a thousand years, and a thousand years are like one day.'[1] For Einstein the physicist, this elasticity of the divine viewpoint becomes everyone's, so that towards the end of his life he was able to declare: 'There is no scientific truth', a key phrase for the dominant position of the uncertainty principle not only in the new physics but in all the other sciences – which is why ethics now finds itself at rock-bottom.

With the primacy currently accorded to light – or to the speed of light perceived as an unsurpassable 'cosmological horizon' – we enter a new order of visibility where the *passing* time of chronology and history is replaced by time which is *exposed* to the absolute speed of light. This shift from the scientific absolutism of Newtonian space and time to Einstein's speed of light is itself revealing [*révélatrice*], in the photographic sense of development [*révélation*].

The famous 'theory of general relativity' is not in fact one, or at least is not as general as it claims to be. And in its space-time continuum it is above all *space-speed* that relativizes the duration and extension of matter for the exclusive benefit of light, omnipotent, omnipresent and invariant in its ultimate rapidity, a living light which reminds us of Bernard de Clairvaux: 'Light is the name of the shadow of the living light.'

With Albert Einstein, but still more with the theorists of an expanding universe, this 'living light' makes it possible to revive the ontological question *par excellence*, the question of God or the beginning of all things, which contemporary physics and astrophysics are attempting to appropriate for themselves.

But let us return to the great scientific prophet of whom Karl Popper tells us: 'Though he may have believed in "scientific" determinism in his formative years, in his later life his determinism was frankly of a religious or metaphysical kind.'[2] For Einstein, as for the theologian Dietrich von Bonhoeffer, 'time is the cycle of light'. The order of time so dear to Kant becomes the order of speed.

As a multitude of local times supersede Newton's global time, the differential order of speed introduces us to a much greater complexity or richness of the three tenses. The 'chronological' movement of past, present and future must now be associated with phenomena of acceleration and deceleration, 'movement of movement', speed changes akin to the phenomena of illumination, or the exposure of the extension and duration of matter to 'daylight' that is not very far at all from that of the metaphysicians. In fact, the order of (absolute) speed is an order of light where the three classical 'times' are reinterpreted in a system that is no longer exactly chronological.

Time – Leibniz's 'order of succession' – becomes with Einstein 'order of exposure', a system of representation of a physical world where future, present and past become interlinked figures of underexposure, exposure and overexposure.

This question of representation in physics soon provoked a serious disagreement between Einstein and Niels Bohr. For the latter, the concept of particle trajectories no longer has any meaning or, at least, is no longer useful in quantum physics, whereas the former rejects the very idea of a physical reality existing independently of all observation. In Einstein, then, the builder of the Potsdam observatory together with the architect Mendelssohn, we see again the significance of the concept of a 'point of view'.

When we realize how important the most diverse vehicles – train, tram, lift, etc. – were for Einstein's insights, we understand how tragic the loss of the concept of passage or trajectory, and therefore of geometry, must have been for him. As the inheritor of Galileo's ballistic relativity, he could not accept the 'conjuring trick' of quantum mechanics.

For Einstein, as for many before him, *speed is useful for seeing*. As qualitative magnitude, as primitive unit of measure, it is prior to any other geometric or chronometric division: *speed is the light of light*. This is confirmed by the various technological experiments with 'exposure time', from Niepce's and Daguerre's dark room through Marey's chronophotography to the present-day elementary particle accelerators which are veritable telescopes of the infinitely small. As a professor of gravitation physics recently explained:

> The best way of directly examining a physical process at atomic or sub-atomic level is to use an accelerated particle beam. For just as light is at once waves and particles (photons), we know that a 'probability wave' is associated with each body in motion. It is this wave associated with accelerated electrons that physicists use in electron microscopes to observe, as with ordinary light, the finest details of the molecules of matter. But as the phenomenon in question becomes smaller, it is necessary to use ever-shorter wavelengths, that is, ever-higher particle beams.[3]

In fact, all the way from the ordinary light of common optical devices (microscope, telescope, etc.) to the latest 'extraordinary' light of the relativist and probabilist optics of electron microscopes, radiotelescopes and other particle accelerators, we have been witnessing a change in physical representation that owes everything to an ever-shorter *exposure time*. This has taken us beyond the time of chronological succession to a chronoscopic or, more exactly, *dromoscopic* order of visibility.

Kant's thesis that time cannot be directly observed, that in the end time is invisible, collapses when we consider that relativity (Einstein's 'point of view theory') corresponds to a kind of photographic (or, more precisely, photonic) 'updating' of the atomic or sub-atomic physical world. Formerly, to let time go by helped us indirectly to see time go by, for the time interval involved a progressive disclosure of events. Today, however, with Einsteinian relativity as generalized 'exposure', it is no longer the progressive extension of time that is useful for seeing, but rather the maximum *intensity* of the speed of light. From now on, the 'light of time' is no longer the light of the sun, of a more or less radiant heavenly body, but the absolute speed of photons as action quantum of light, as yardstick and outer limit of the perceived world.

Yesterday, *passing* time corresponded to the *extensive time* of calendars, and this fully justified Kant's thesis of invisibility. But now the time of *instant exposure* corresponds to the *intensive* chronoscopic time of the 'relativistic eternal present', an integral optics resembling the ubiquitousness and simultaneity of the divine gaze, the *totum simul* when the successive moments of time are equally present in a single perception that makes of them a landscape of events.[4]

Thus the 'daytime' of general relativity is no longer that of solar revolution but that of *photon resolution* – a resolution which ultimately permits the general readability of duration, the visibility of time, as ocular accommodation or high-resolution lenses increase the clarity of a snapshot.

We can understand a little better now Einstein's bewilderment in the early days of quantum physics. For he had tirelessly elaborated an aesthetic of relativist representation of the cosmos, and now he was suddenly faced with its opposite, an aesthetic of quantum disappearance that was to light what Dirac's anti-matter already was to matter: namely, an 'anti-light' in which the geometry of elementary particle trajectories blurred his famous four-dimensional continuum. In fact, Heisenberg's uncertainty principle that underpinned quantum mechanics led to a kind of dis-continuum where the number of dimensions constantly increased or fluctuated,[5] so that Niels Bohr finally concluded in 1927: 'A description in space and time must largely be given up [. . .]. The wish for intuitive representation through images in space and time is not justified.'

Thus, much to Einstein's displeasure, by doing away with the object independent of observation, quantum theory led to a ban on representation that made it necessary to give up the traditional concepts of space, time and causality.

Since the 'objects' under examination were no longer considered real objects but, in Heisenberg's words, 'subject-objects', *the indeterminacy principle thus led to abandonment of the reality principle.* For if quantum phenomena no longer occur in relativist space-time, it is because they are no longer inscribed within any order of succession or spatio-temporal position, but only within an order of ultra-relativist (instantaneous) exposure in the records from CERN acceleration tracks. In those experimental hallucinations, the physicist is a little like someone content to observe and count light signals coming to him through the night, while refusing to believe there is someone else there with a lamp, or that there is no lamp there at all but only a distant beam, a quantum dazzling or vertigo, a pure revelation from the Beyond!

This explains the race for high energy, the construction of giant accelerators like the LEP collision track 27 kilometres in circumference at CERN in Geneva, or the SLAC linear accelerator at Stanford, California, or the proposal on the part of some physicists impatient at experimental delays *to build a particle accelerator that circles the earth, or even to build one in circumterrestrial space* so that the brightness of the speed of light is increased still more. This dawning of a subliminal day no longer has any point in common with the course from the rising to the setting sun; it is a time without duration, an intensive time capable of supplanting the extensive time of calendars and history.

* * *

'The perfect objectivity of space-time and the macroscopic events it contains', we hear from Olivier Costa de Beauregard, 'is most likely an illusion, just like the objectivity one tends to attribute to the concept of probability in its frequential aspect. In fact, neither "space-time" nor "probability" is totally objective, nor totally subjective either; they are indissolubly both at once.'[6]

In the same disenchanted vein, he eventually introduces the idea of 'stereo-spatiality' to resolve the cosmological dispute between quantum physics and Einsteinian relativity: on the one hand, there is 'exo-space', the familiar space-time of macroscopic events; on the other, there is the 'endo-space' of microscopic quantum events. What happens, then, to the concept of *physical magnitudes* or dimensions of the cosmos, since the concept of energy now replaces distance – these two quantities being linked by Heisenberg's uncertainty principle? Are we to understand that, alongside the *dual spatiality* proposed by Costa de Beauregard, there is also room for a *dual temporality*, one infinitely small and one infinitely large?

If that really were the case, it would clarify the intuitive concept of time without duration, a time of intensity short of Einsteinian space-time, and the quest in microphysics for elementary particles or billionths of a second (nanosecond, picosecond, femtosecond . . .) would take on an opposite meaning to that of the current attempt at temporal regression (the famous astrophysical search for the first instants of the universe).

In apparent confirmation of this, some scientists explain:

In this perspective, to understand the origins of the universe is to understand the instability of an original 'quantum nothing'. Fifteen billion years ago, the universe sprang out of 'nothing' and our universal clock started ticking, but the time that defines this clock – the time that goes by in the *curved* universe – is not the time associated with the *flat* space-time of the original void. As in the case of a black hole, the distinctive relationship between these two times leads to a paradoxical conclusion: namely, that *the universe has existed for a finite time, and it has sprung out of quantum nothingness since an infinite time.*[7]

In fact, the 'infinitely small' of duration, such as experiments in intensive acceleration seem to allow, modifies our perception of temporality: *the race for absolute intensity of time turns reality inside out like a glove.* The yardstick of duration is no longer really 'duration' but, paradoxically, the infinite and constant deepening of 'the instant'; the origin of the universe seems within reach of instruments (if not the future space telescope), while the infinitely small of the instant appears out of reach.

In this doubling of the infinite, the ban on representation, the cosmological blindness, becomes central. On the one hand, the infinitely 'large' of relativist space-time seems accessible to our measuring instruments (radiotelescope, spectroscope, etc.); on the other hand, the infinitely 'small' of ultra-relativist space-speed is for ever inaccessible, because experts tell us there would have to be a particle accelerator the size of our galaxy (or even of the universe) to have any hope of contemplating the Beyond of time!

In trying to reconstitute this cosmogonic jigsaw in which the doubling of time causes the doubling of infinity, we observe a strange 'conception of the world' where the macrocosm is finite and the microcosm has no end, where macroscopic space-time is perceptible not in spite of its size but thanks to its very gigantism, while microscopic space-speed is imperceptible for the opposite reason. On the one hand, we observe an *extensive time* of the infinitely large of duration (space-time), which is calculated in billions of years. On the other hand, an *intensive time* of the infinitely small of time (space-speed) is counted in billionths of a second, and here the theological question of Genesis, or, if you prefer, the ontological question of the first minutes of the universe as posed by Nobel prizewinner Steven Weinberg, is in danger of losing its meaning, at least as far as the 'beginning of time' is concerned.

For if there really is an infinitely small of time as there is one of space (as the theory of relativity requires), the first minute of the universe is infinite and a beginning of time has to be sought deep inside the absolute intensity of the instant.

In this interpretation, then, what meet at the junction (interface) of space-time and space-speed are a beginning hidden in the infinitesimal of *present time* and a beginning hidden in the infinitely large of the longest duration of *past time* – two 'beginnings' for a single Genesis, or two 'cosmological origins' for two beginnings? In a thesis completed in 1933, *Le Temps et l'éternité chez Plotin et saint Augustin*, Jean Guitton writes:

> As the instant is essentially a middle, it is impossible to assume an especially favoured instant that is an end without being a beginning or a beginning without also being an end. We see how absurd it is to envisage a birth of time in the manner of Plato.

It is this relativity, this general elasticity of duration, which upholders of mystical experience sense and reveal. If, as the apostle says, 'With the Lord one day is as a thousand years, and a thousand years are as one day,' for the convinced relativist *a billionth of a second is like fifteen billion years* and the fifteen billion years that are supposed to separate us from the beginning of the cosmos are no more than one nanosecond, that is, one billionth of a second. Hence the childishness of that astrophysical quest for 'the beginning of all things', just when the search is developing (especially in microphysics) for the greatest accelerations of all.

Thus, Albert Einstein's refusal to accept the principle of an expanding universe – that is, the ideology of the evolutionist model applied to the cosmos – cannot simply be explained in terms of the intellectual sclerosis of an old determinist genius refusing to abandon his 'stationary' model. Rather, it allows us to appreciate the real value of his testament-like pronouncement that *there is no scientific truth*.

For the theorist of general relativity (1915), the theory of an expanding universe – suspected as early as 1922 by the Soviet physicist Alexander Friedmann, and confirmed seven years later by the American astronomer Edwin Hubble – leads to *a cosmological optical illusion*. The general flight of heavenly bodies, and the famous red shift in the light of galaxies, certainly leads to a perspectival *vanishing point*, but not at all – as the physicists Lemaître and Gamov claimed in the thirties and forties – to an original *starting point* when the necessary conditions for cosmic reality one day supposedly came together and bore fruit. Today, in a manner reminiscent of the Russian egg-doll, this view is leading some to seek the final 'truth of truths' behind the universe, the opposite of the relativity principle dear to the old Jewish scientist![8]

At any event, catastrophe is becoming the alpha and omega of contemporary cosmogony. Whether as Big Bang or Big Crunch, physicists are trapped by their cosmological logic into giving *accident* the primary importance that they used to accord to substance. Thus, whatever is said or done, accident is absolute and necessary, substance relative and contingent. For materialists, who are convinced 'anti-creationists', *accident has become the secular form of the miracle*!

* * *

In September 1985, four astronomers at the Toulouse observatory discovered a *luminous arc*. Two years later, in November 1987, the same astronomers irrefutably demonstrated that this was an 'Einstein ring', an optical effect better known by the name 'gravitational lens' and predicted long ago by the general theory of relativity.

After readings were taken at the Hawaii observatory in 1986, and above all at the Silla observatory in Chile, the scientific team finally concluded that the luminous arc was nothing other than the deformed image of a spiral galaxy six or seven billion light-years away. Between this galaxy and ourselves, at a distance of some five billion light-years, the vast Abell 70 'cluster of galaxies' plays the role both of a distorting lens and of a magnifying glass.

Rather as an optical glass deflects rays of light, such an enormous mass of matter may also deflect the light from a celestial body. As experts wrote in the press at the time: 'This phenomenon of gravitational optics should enable researchers to discover other remote and hitherto undetectable galaxies.'[9] A luminous arc, a gravitational ring – why not also a sphere, a *dromosphere*?

If a cluster of galaxies can cause such an effect of kinematic optics that a galaxy comparable to our own Milky Way becomes visible, how could we fail to suspect that all the matter in the universe acts similarly upon our vision of the world?

As everyone knows, light is a form of energy and its mass is influenced by the gravitational field – hence the bending of light beams in the illusion of relativist optics. The shortest route light can take is always either a 'curve' or a 'large circle', determined by the non-Euclidean geometry of the field, and the structure of this gravitational field is itself determined by the mass and speed of the different 'bodies in gravitation': stars, planets, galaxies or galaxy clusters. The geometry or topology of general relativity, that is, the very structure of our universe, must therefore be defined by the sum of matter in relative movement that it contains. Now, given that light travels at the same speed in every direction, the *visible* arc or circle is never anything other than a section of a larger cosmological ensemble, an *indivisible* topological ensemble that might be called the 'dromosphere' (that is, the sphere of speeds relative to the final and absolute speed of light, the universal constant determining the *cosmological horizon* or visibility cone of astronomical appearances). The 'expansion of the universe', then, is simply the most spectacular illustration of the kinematic optics of general relativity – an optics in which the concrete illusion of the moment, always prevailing over scientific truth, is the very reality of the heavenly bodies glimpsed here and there in that zone of phenomenal emergence permitted by the limiting speed.

For if speed is not at all a 'phenomenon' but only the relation *between* phenomena (relativity itself), we might adapt Bernard de Clairvaux by stating that light is the name for the shadow of absolute speed, or, to be more precise, that the speed of rays of light (geometrical optics) is the name for the shadow of the speed of light of electro-magnetic waves (wave optics). With light energy thus divided into light and speed of diffusion of light, we would be led to conclude that speed is useful *for seeing*, but above all that it makes 'light' visible *even before the objects (or phenomena) that it illuminates*.[10]

This precisely is the *dromosphere*: not so much expansion of the universe 'brought to light' by the famous red shift in the spectrum, but a purely relativist recognition that it is *speed* – not just light and its spectral analysis – which enlightens the universe of perceptible and measurable phenomena.

On the one hand, direct light of the sun's rays and electric lamps. On the other hand, indirect light of electro-magnetic waves which are useful for communicating, for *relating* more than illuminating, for *bringing to light* things (quantity, quality) to be apprehended in the instant of looking at them.

What is involved here is not simply a metaphor of speed and its 'light', but a veritable doubling of perception such as Einstein and a few others have proposed.

For nearly a century now, *to save phenomena is to save their speed of apperception*. In 1905 Einstein's 'point of view theory' brought a way of seeing the physical world that owed virtually everything to the absolute character of 'speed' as a cosmological limit replacing absolute Newtonian 'time' and 'space'. A kind of eternal dromological present became the figure of a physics where speed suddenly emerged as the *life* of phenomena, or more exactly their precarious *survival* without which science would instantly vanish and physics would give way to metaphysics alone.

Effraction, refraction, diffraction: Newton's two generic absolutes were replaced in the early years of the century by Einstein's *speed* and *light* (the *c* constant). Later, with Louis de Broglie, acceptance of the 'wave/corpuscle' division gave contemporary physics a still clearer dual character, which quantum mechanics and Heisenberg's uncertainty principle extended into the well-known paradox that we can know the speed of a particle but not its position – or its position but not its speed.

It was a fundamental dichotomy, deriving this time from the distinction not simply between matter and light but between wave and particle.

Here our use of the term 'dromosphere' for what has previously been called 'expansion of the universe' is merely an attempt to extend this tendency. By thus establishing the indirect light of speed in place of the customary importance accorded to direct light, we are trying not just to take seriously the kinematic character of relativist optics but, above all, to give due and serious weight to the aberrations, or, more precisely, to the *dromoscopic* illusion, recently revealed by a number of astronomers in the area of gravitational optics, where it is agreed that gravity is propagated at the same speed as photons.

Everyone has known for a long time that the starry night is never more than an illusion, since no astronomer is in a position to tell us whether the remote source of the nocturnal scintillation is still active. Only recently, however, has this first illusion due to the finite speed of light been coupled with the still stranger one of *dromospheric mirages* which, after the fashion of atmospheric mirages, multiply the number of stars on show.

Not only does the 'magnifying-glass effect' of gravitational lenses allow us to see the most distant heavenly bodies that we ought never to see; it actually makes us see double! Intoxication with speed is no longer just a hollow expression. The deflection of light within the gravitational field, due to the proximity of major cosmic masses, means that astronomers no longer believe their own eyes, or even those of telescopes or radiotelescopes.

Nowadays, the aim of the observatories' nightly search is not so much to count the number of stars as to uncover the multiple illusions and angular distortions of gravitational optics – to count not phenomena but those numerous *epiphenomena* which preoccupy astrophysicists (wrongly doubled or even tripled stars, binary quasars or pulsars, gravitational and purely relativist mirages). Thus the refraction of light due to universal gravitation is gradually taking over from the innocently observed light of cosmic sources, while we await experimental confirmation of the famous 'gravity waves' and the inauguration of a *gravitational astronomy*.

Since there is no part of the 'heavens' that does not show some angular deformation, the sky of the astronomers and astrophysicists is never more than a gigantic 'refraction effect', a cosmic illusion due to the relativity of celestial motion, so that only the most high-performing instruments are thought capable of measuring the scale of this gravitational deformation and thus, after the fashion of opticians' spectacles, of correcting our 'vision of the world'.

'The more perfect telescopes become, the more stars there will be,' wrote Gustave Flaubert, not without a touch of humour. In fact, the more perfect astronomic and radio-astronomic instruments become, the more we will discover with astonishment that the indirect light of speed is the main source of light in cosmic space. In this temporal illumination, the *astrophysics of illusions* will probably take over from the astronomy of actual objects; then the universe of the kinematic optics of general relativity and the future 'astronomy of gravity waves' will become identified with a vast dromospheric illusion analogous to the familiar ones in the earth's atmosphere.

It may even be legitimate to suppose that the increasingly high resolution of macrocosmic images, like that of the microcosm in the recent past, will lead to a final 'loss of vision' comparable to that which quantum physics already illustrates, thereby generalizing the terms of the debate between Niels Bohr and Albert Einstein concerning the importance of observation in physics: that is, ultimately, the status of experimental visibility.

'The separation of past, present and future, here and there, no longer has any meaning except as a visual illusion,' wrote Einstein in a letter of condolences to the family of his friend Michele Besso – condolences, surely, for classical experimental physics and its schema of visibility!

If, in interstellar space-time, there is objectively neither up nor down, future nor past, but only a present illustrated by the simple presence at one point of a potential observer,[11] then the sphere of emergence of phenomena (or, if you like, the cone of light) has such

a 'reality effect' only because of the relativist approximation of the
field and not by virtue of any (ocular or optical) 'objectivity' stemming from an external source of light, such as experimenters
demanded long ago in the Age of Enlightenment.

In the end, the dromological effraction of *the time of light* (of time-
light) is but a continuation of the morphological effraction of the
space of matter resulting from the discoveries of atomic and sub-
atomic physics.

Minkowski's questioning of the old geometric tripartition, Man-
delbrot's and a few others' more recent rejection of the ancient
concept of 'entire dimension', are leading us towards a veritable 'disintegration of the old conceptual frameworks' of physics and astrophysics. After the multidimensional theory of Kaluza-Klein, it is the
theory of *phase space* or cosmic cords (the fibred space of the latest
mathematics) which is carrying still further the disintegration of both
'extension' and 'duration', 'position' and 'velocity'.

Whatever materialists may think, the relativity of mystics helps to
clarify the relativity of contemporary 'micro' or 'macro' physics: the
notion that at the end of the tunnel of science *there is nothing to see*;
that geometric or wave optics is never anything other than a staging
of the kinematic illusion. Actually this was well known to Einstein,
the man who toppled the space and time of matter from their throne
and established the absolute rule not of light but of speed, an absolute speed, we should remember, which is shared by universal gravitation.

Rationally speaking, to take relativity seriously is to pass objectively beyond the status of visibility inherited from the Enlightenment – a project already largely sketched out by the statisticians of
the 'probability calculus' responsible for the quantum discoveries.

To say, as we now should, that the speed of light in a 'vacuum' is
the new *absolute* replacing that of the extension and duration of
matter is indirectly to assert that *relativity is absolute and necessary
while truth is contingent and limited* – the truth not just of the sense-
appearances of aesthetics, but also of the various techniques of
measurement and observation.

Here is how the young Einstein put it in 1916:

> The concept 'true' does not tally with the assertions of pure geometry, because by
> the word 'true' we are eventually in the habit of designating always the corre-
> spondence with a real object; geometry, however, is not concerned with the rela-
> tion of the ideas involved in it to objects of experience, but only with the logical
> connection of these ideas among themselves.[12]

This relativist detachment would affect one object of scientific experience after another, up to the famous dialogue of 1927 between Bohr and Einstein concerning the very usefulness of the concept of trajectory (positions or speeds, to be sure, but nothing between them). The recent development of the *static optics* of computer-generated imagery will complete this exile, helping to replace scientists' 'thought experiments' with 'computer experiments' and, little by little, to make the digital optics of computer graphics prevail over the analogic optics of customary visibility.

For if speed is not a 'phenomenon' but the relationship between phenomena, the speed of computer calculation is today achieving what the geometric optics of lenses had been achieving since the time of Galileo.[13]

That first 'absolute speed machine' largely prefigured the wave optics of our modern electronic instruments. Nor is that all, since chance now affects thought processes and the advance of scientific theories themselves. If truth is 'limited' and relativity absolute and necessary (like Aristotle's substance), the question for us is to recognize this frontier, this 'limitation' of truth. But in fact the answer is contained in the question: what limits the truth of facts is still that 'speed' which is the measure of both phenomena and epiphenomena. Relativity is never more than this absolute limitation of scientific objectivity by the 'enigma of time', no longer just the extensive, passing time of centuries and Eternity, as in Saint Augustine, but the *intensive* (exposed) time of infinitesimal duration permitted by the new technologies.

It is as if absolute yet finite speed was also the transfer accident between one end and another of the time span, including that of human knowledge.

Listen again to Einstein, this time much later in life: 'What distinguishes a correct theory from a false theory? Its *period of validity*!' A few years or decades for the former, a few days or months for the latter. But what follows if, as we are entitled to do, we acknowledge the role of 'calculation speed' not only in verifying hypotheses but also in crucially yielding an active optics that complements the passive optics of lenses – that is, an active 'digital' or statistical optics which favours not only foresight, as any mathematical calculation does, but actual 'clairvoyance' of the results of calculation? If we acknowledge this role, we must also contemplate a *gradual restriction of the period of validity of scientific theories*, not because of any incapacity on the part of scientists but because of the overcapacity of their means: that is, simply because of the rapidly increasing number of calculations and the extent of 'indirect' observation that owes everything to the 'light' of speed (hypothesis-checking speed which ultimately limits the validity of laws). There will come a day, and it is not very far off, when the limits of rational visibility will be reached and the very plausibility of our knowledge in physics and astrophysics will disappear – a falling away of the very necessity of external references, as the rise of quantum mechanics foreshadowed. This 'death', or at least this *relativist disappearance*, is linked to the discrediting of passive (direct) optics to the benefit of active or even 'activist' (indirect) optics. *Eye death* of the scientific researcher here represents for physicists the same crisis of conscience that Nietzsche's death (or relative disappearance) of God provoked in metaphysicians, relativist renunciation of faith in perception corresponding to objectivist renunciation of religious faith.

What has happened to art will soon happen to science: not only silence (as the astronomer Michel Cassé fears) but *blindness*[14] – a paradoxical blindness due to the excessive speed of light which will finally rob us of external referents. As a teleological conclusion, we might quote here Paul of Tarsus: 'Visible things have only a time; invisible ones are eternal.' It is the eternity of duration, of course, but also the eternity of the infinitely small time which, though escaping our understanding, is constantly made available to us by our various technologies.

Already in the 1930s, a decade so fruitful in changes, Kurt Gödel's theorem shook the rationalist edifice by *mathematically* establishing that there are 'true' propositions which can be neither demonstrated nor invalidated, since the theory of numbers contains a principle of absolute incompleteness. Amid this crisis of logic and mathematics, Alan Turing developed *a contrario* in the forties the principle of the 'thought machine', a precursor of what would later become electronic computing. But what Turing could hardly have suspected was that his famous invention would lead thirty years later to the emergence of the *vision machine*. This automaton providing digital perception called into question not only the axiomatic foundations of mathematics, as Gödel had done before, but all the processes of knowledge acquisition itself. The power of the 'digital machines' descended from Turing's has never consisted in anything other than their speed of calculation, but this power allows them to apprehend information from the surrounding milieu, that is, *to see, to perceive in our place*, so that the scientist today, like the artist yesterday, becomes a mere 'demonstrator of equipment', since computers now make it possible for scientists to *imagine* their own theories.

* * *

> In the universe there is no distinction between the two directions of time, just as in space there is no above and no below. But just as, at certain points of the earth's surface, we may call 'below' the direction of the centre of the earth, so a living organism that finds itself in such a world at a given moment may define the 'direction' of time as passing from the least probable to the most probable state, the former being the past and the latter the future.

In this reply to Zermelo dating from 1897 (one year after Eugène Promio's invention of the travelling shot), Ludwig Boltzmann identified *the present* with the presence of a *living* observer at a certain place and time. He thus related the apperception of passing time with metabolic aliveness, as if the present were identical *à la* Bergson simply with the consciousness of passing time – as if, apart from 'mortals', time had no specific duration, no 'quantity' and no 'quality' distinguishing Before from After, just as interstellar extension does not distinguish Above and Below, man (or, rather, animate creatures) being the measure of all things.

This is still the basis for what is called the *anthropic principle*, which regards the existence of any observer as inseparable from the existence of rationally observed phenomena. But let us return to the 'arrow of time' and Boltzmann's analysis, which does not raise the question of the centre of intensive time and only clearly poses that of extensive time. There is a complete impasse concerning the very probability of an infinitely 'small' of time.

Only in 1905 did Einstein's discovery of the absolute speed of light in a vacuum fundamentally alter the debate between Zermelo and Boltzmann. For if the centre of extensive time really is 'the present', that is, 'the living', then it must be accepted that the aliveness of any animate organism (animal) is its alertness or *vivacity*, or in other words the schema of temporality of being, the *metabolic speed* with which the observer acquires information. The living organism here has the function of a centre of relativist space-time; it is quite impossible to separate the observer from the thing observed, relativist non-separability having largely anticipated the principle of quantum non-separability.

The 'centre' of extensive time is therefore (through the observer's present state) the relative speed or *vivacity* of the animate being (its age, health, performance in various areas). The centre of chronological time (past, present, future) is therefore always the relativist temporality of being present here and now. In fact, this speed of the living present (of the presence of being) which marks out Boltzmann's Before and After carries us into what might be called the *axis of intensive time*, the second axis of time's arrow that is continually lengthened by our various optical or electro-optical, acoustic or electro-acoustic, means of acquiring information.

Now, this new question of the infinitely small of time (nanosecond, picosecond, femtosecond), which involves a veritable disintegration of the time of light comparable to the disintegration of the space of matter (nuclear fission or fusion), is itself a scientific question going beyond the traditional three-dimensional investigations of the *instant* within classical philosophy.

For the present instant is no longer simply a 'lapse of time'; it opens up the possibility of an infinitely short duration containing the equivalent of what is already contained in the infinitely 'long' duration and infinitely 'large' space of the perceived cosmos which is limited (for the observer) by the absolute yet finite speed of light in the vacuum.

In the axis of intensive time, the second paradoxical axis of all 'duration', the speed of light is therefore the impassable *cosmological horizon*, as the so-called beginning of space-time, the Big Bang, already is in the axis of extensive time.

The third kind of interval, the (zero sign) 'light' interval, thus takes its place alongside the two others: the 'space' interval (minus sign) and the 'time' interval (plus sign). It constitutes the *dromosphere*, that is, not only the 'visibility cone' mentioned earlier, but the sphere of perception of the very reality of all phenomena, beginning with the purely relativist reality effect of the space and time intervals which played such a part in our history and our geometry.

The time of light, or more exactly *time-light*, is thus the 'centre of time'. The intensive time of light and universal gravitation should now be the basis for any study of duration and extension, of the extensive time of the matter of objects and places. It is on the basis of this *intensive present* that attempts should be made to observe what people agree to call reality.

The absolute speed of light in a vacuum, the zero-sign interval, is thus 'absolute lighting', the disclosure of both the extension and duration of phenomena, the 'inter-viewing' of reality.

As the centre or, more precisely, the medium of time, absolute speed is the limit of the real. But if speed is this *medium*, objective reality exists only in and through it, through *relativist mediation* which limits the concepts of the infinitely large and the infinitely small, of the space-time continuum, of the two intervals that would be nothing (for us observers present here) without the third interval. Thus, we may now legitimately mention not only the passing time of chronology and history, but also the time which exposes itself, as space does, to the light of the universal constant of speed.

It is the exposure time of *chronoscopy* which complements the classical *chronological* time of succession, so that the light of time serves to expose, and then to overexpose, physical reality.

'Everything visible is only a parabola' was Goethe's view. Yes, but it is parabolic in the sense of those mirrors which – thanks to the geometric optics of their rays – make light converge so that we can see what the real ultimately is, that 'present instant' whose depth has no other limit than the speed of emission of the 'reality waves' that make up not only the image but also the thing represented.

Notes

1. 2 Peter 3.8.

2. Karl Popper, *The Open Universe: An Argument for Indeterminism*, London: Routledge, 1988, p. 89.

3. Abhaq Ashtekar, 'La Gravitation quantique', *La Recherche*, November 1984.

4. Louis O. Mink's commentary on Boethius, quoted by Paul Ricoeur.

5. The Kaluza/Klein theory, for example, is an attempt within a quantum framework to unify the basic forces of nature in a space-time with more than four dimensions.

6. Olivier Costa de Beauregard, *La Notion de temps*, Paris: Éd. Hermann, 1963.

7. Edgard Gunzig and Isabelle Stengers, 'Mort et résurrection de l'horloge universelle', *L'Art et le temps*, Brussels 1984.

8. We should note, however, that the 'evolutionary' conception has itself evolved and that 'expansion' or 'dilation' is no longer thought an appropriate term to describe the *dromosphere*. 'The geometry of the universe, its metrics, evolve in such a way that the distance between any two points regularly increases over time, exactly as general relativity predicted.' Nicolas Prantzos and Michel Cassé, 'L'Avenir de l'univers', *La Recherche*, June 1984.

9. Dominique Leglu, 'Quatre astronomes toulousains prouvent l'existence d'un anneau d'Einstein', *Libération*, 3 November 1987.

10. The anthropic principle: no observer, no light.

11. As Ludwig Boltzmann clearly explained in 1897, in his reply to Zermelo.

12. Albert Einstein, *Relativity: The Special and the General Theory*, London: Methuen, 1960, p. 2.

13. Galileo was the first *scientific* relativist – hence his conflict with the religious relativism of the Church of Rome.

14. See the final chapter of Paul Virilio, *The Vision Machine*, London: British Film Institute, 1994.

4

ENVIRONMENT CONTROL

I am not looking for anything. I am here.

Philippe Soupault

What are the implications for the transparency of air, water and glass, for the 'real space' of the things surrounding us, when the 'real-time' *interface* supersedes the classical *interval*, and distance suddenly gives way to power of emission and instant reception? What happens, in the end, when classical optical communication is replaced by electro-optical *commutation*?

If repeated use of the prefix 'de-' (as in decentralization, deregulation, deconstruction, etc.) has set its seal on the times, we may perhaps add another term – *derangement*: not only of sense-appearances but of transparency itself, a 'transparency' with nothing beyond, which has nothing in common with the density of any material or even of the earth's atmosphere.

If transparency may be defined as 'that which light can easily pass through', or as 'that which allows us clearly to perceive objects through its very density' (a window-pane, for example), it changes its nature with the new concept of *real-time interface*, since now it is the transparency not of light rays (solar or electrical) but only of the speed of elementary particles (electron, photon . . .) propagated at the very speed of light.

Light remains the only discloser of sense-appearances; but now it is its *speed* which discloses or makes things visible, to the detriment of sunlight or the artificial light of electricity.

Transparency, then, no longer just refers to the appearance of objects that become visible at the moment of looking. Now, suddenly, it refers to the appearances instantly transmitted over a distance – which is why we have suggested speaking of the *trans-appearance* of real time, and not just the transparency of real space. 'Live' transmission of the appearance of things is now superseding the old real-space transparency of air, water or lens glass.

In fact, this move beyond the direct transparency of materials is principally due to the emergence of a new, *active optics* through the recent development of optical electronics and radio-electrical vision, to the detriment of the previously supreme *passive optics* of telescope, microscope or camera lenses. In other words, it is mainly due to the application of wave optics right beside classical *geometrical optics*. Thus, much as a non-Euclidean or topological geometry is now available alongside Euclidean geometry, the passive optics of the geometry of camera or telescope lenses now has right beside it a 'tele-topological' *active optics* of electro-optical waves.

Furthermore, in parallel to the instant transmission of a radio-like 'video signal', optical properties have recently become attached to computers through the digitalization of transmitted images. The optical correction of appearances is no longer just a matter of the geometry of camera lenses, but now involves point-by-point (pixel-by-pixel) calculation of the picture through a computer linked to the transmitter, digitalization offering a better definition of appearances, as in the most recent 'adjustable optics' telescopes where the lens does not have to be flawless because the *calculation speed of computer graphics* achieves the optical correction of light rays. Here again we see the supremacy of the speed of light over the illuminating capacity of its rays.

On the one hand, the speed of electrons and photons indirectly lights up what remains distant, thanks to video reception of the broadcast appearances (videoscopy being a great improvement upon classical telescopy). On the other hand, the speed of electronic pixel calculation accelerates the definition or clarity of the picture, overshadowing the optical quality even of the soft lenses of new telescopes. Thus, it is less light than speed which helps us to see, to measure and therefore to conceive the reality of appearances.

Now acceleration is useful not so much for easy movement over distance as for clear vision or apperception, high definition of reality entirely depending upon speed of transmission of appearances, and not just on transparency of the atmosphere or various materials.

To grasp the real importance of the 'analyser' that speed, especially audiovisual speed, now represents, we must again turn to the philosophical definition: 'Speed is not a phenomenon but *a relationship between phenomena*.' In other words it is the very *relativity* or transparency of the reality of appearances, but a 'spatio-temporal transparency' that here supersedes the spatial transparency of the linear geometry of optical lenses – hence the term *trans-appearance* to designate the transmitted electronic appearances, whatever the space interval separating them from the observer. This subject or *subjugated* observer thus becomes inseparable from the observed object, because of the very immediacy of the interface, of the aptly named 'terminal' that perfects the extension and duration of a world reduced to man–machine commutation, where the 'spatial depth' of perspectival geometry suddenly gives way to the 'temporal depth' of a *real-time perspective* superseding the old real-space perspective of the Renaissance.

* * *

Let us now look at a few technological examples of this new *real-time optics*. Researchers at NASA and the Ophthalmology Institute at Johns Hopkins University, Baltimore, have recently developed a pair of revolutionary spectacles: two miniature lenses fitted to a frame transmit images by optical fibre to two minute video cameras fitted at the height of the imperfectly sighted patient. The electronically processed image is then sent back to the spectacles, which have screens instead of corrective lenses. This optical-electronic system, soon to be marketed in the United States, automatically adjusts images to the particular sight of the wearer, who thus has a bright and clear-seeming image before his or her eyes.

This system, which has been tested on remote-controlled robots, is one by-product of military research into the 'vision machine' of the future. In fact, recent work on the automation of perception has the declared aim of replacing immediate with indirect, *assisted* perception, where the speed of electrons will be of greater advantage than the light of the sun's rays or electric bulbs.

Thus, while the spectacular research of a Scott Fisher at NASA is developing an *interactive* virtual environment helmet (that is, a portable simulator akin to the one on board fighter aircraft), these video spectacles are more modest testimony to the coming transformation of ocular optics into a truly everyday electro-optics. The look of direct vision is thus ceding to a real-time, radio-electrical *industrialization of vision* capable one day of standing in for, if not supplanting, our observation of the environment. The direct light of the sun, candles or electric lamps will gradually make way for the not just artificial but indirect light of electronics or photonics, following the example of those windowless Japanese apartments that are *bathed in sunshine* by means of optical fibres.

In the next century, said Timothy Leary, whoever controls the screen will control consciousness – and indeed, contrary to a widespread belief, the very first interactivity is not the remote control or the touch-operated screen but the inter-visibility of various filming devices, what we might call *opto-activity*. This links up or merges three kinds of image: the virtual image of consciousness, the ocular and optical image of the look, and the electro-optical or radio-electrical image of video computing.

This is the point of our proposed concept of *trans-appearance*, rather than just transparency.

The indirect light of various electro-optical (and electro-acoustic) prostheses competes with the direct light of classical optics. The customary distinction between natural and artificial light is then coupled with an unaccustomed one between direct and indirect light.

For whereas the light radiating from an electric lamp or the sun gives rise to *ordinary* transparency, the indirect light of electrons, photons and various devices gives rise to an *extra-ordinary* transparency in which the real time of the image prevails over the real space of vision, and instantly transmitted appearances supersede the usual illumination of places.

This light-acceleration function is clearly displayed in *light-intensifying* cameras or binoculars, where rare nocturnal photons are multiplied to give a considerable increase in ambient brightness.

Thus, the time-frequency of light has suddenly become the determining factor in the apperception of phenomena, to the detriment of the space-frequency of matter. From now on, the speed of light has the upper hand over sunshine or ordinary lighting.

* * *

But let us return to the origins of this situation – to photography.

In his conversations with Paul Gsell, who thought he had irrefutable evidence of the photography of movement, Auguste Rodin objected: 'No, it is the artist who is truthful and photography which is false. For in reality *time does not stop*, and if the artist succeeds in producing the impression of a gesture performed over several instants, his work is certainly much less conventional than a scientific image in which time is suddenly suspended.'

This key statement, later taken up by Maurice Merleau-Ponty,[1] is worth some consideration. The time in question here is the usual linear time of *chronology*, which never stops but keeps flowing on. But the really new contribution of photosensitive techniques – which Rodin seems not to have noticed – was that they defined no longer a passing time but rather an exposure time which 'surfaces' (if we may dare put it like that) and thus succeeds the time of classical historical succession.

The time of 'taking photographs' is thus from the start *light-time*. The *time* interval (plus sign) and the *space* interval (minus sign: with the same name as the film's inscription surface) are inscribed only thanks to *light*, to that third kind of interval whose zero sign indicates absolute speed.

The exposure time of the photographic plate is therefore nothing but *exposure of the time* (space-time) of its photosensitive material to the speed of light, that is, to the frequency of the photon-bearing wave.

Thus, the sculptor Rodin also does not see that it is only the *surface* of the negative (negative interval) which stops the *time* of the representation of movement. When the instant photogram permitted the invention of the cinematographic sequence, *time no longer stopped*. The reel of recorded film, and later the 'real-time' video cassette of constant surveillance, illustrate this invention of *continuous light-time* (the most important in science since the discovery of fire) in which *indirect* light supersedes the direct light of the sun or the Edison lamp, as the latter itself once superseded daylight.

From the eighteenth and nineteenth centuries on, time is thus no longer so much a problem of more or less rapid *ageing*; it is above all a question of more or less intensive *lighting* – the famous Age of Enlightenment obviously well deserving its name.

This seems to be the main philosophical contribution of Niepce's invention, but also, above all, of that *snap-shot* which eventually made possible Marey's chronophotography and the later emergence of real-time technologies in which two times (the real and the deferred) take over from the customary three, with the future appearing in the computer and systems programming of the 'vision machine'.[2]

By way of confirming the emergence of this *light-time*, let us note that picture-taking became shorter and shorter between the hours-long pose of early photography and the invention of the snap-shot. Similarly, in the cinema, the reduction in the through-time of one frame (from 17 f.p.s. to 24 f.p.s. and then 30 f.p.s.) was for many years

– until television really began to take off – offset by *spatial elongation* of the film and therefore of its projection. This spatial elongation has been combined with temporal shortening, from early flash cinematography to present-day videoclips.

For more than a hundred and fifty years, then, temporal speed-up has led to advances in what still and moving photography represent. It is the 'light of time' – or, if you prefer, the time of *speed-light* – which has illuminated the world around us, to such a point that it seems to be no longer a mere 'means of representation' akin to painting, sculpture or theatre, but a veritable 'means of information'. Hence the forward surge of information technology – from the days of electronic calculators to the 'computer-generated image', the digitalized video or radio signal, and 'high-resolution vision' (or high-fidelity sound), where the only unit of measure is the 'bits per second' designating the quantity of information conveyed by a 'message', and *the image is left as the most sophisticated form of information*. Let us recall that the true measure of time is not, as most people think, the number of years, months or hours that have passed, but the alternation of day and night, the order of daytime and its absence. Even if calculation (whether astronomical or economic) is a kind of *foresight*, even if the totting up of ephemeris and calendar days has signposted human history, it is no less true that shadow and light are at the very origin of *time information*, the yardstick of duration that is not only quantifiable but also qualifiable. Thanks to the theory of Shannon and a few others, we can see that there are actually two kinds of information: *knowledge* information and *organization* information.

Now, in both these cases, the intervals of passing time have grown ever more precise – from the hours of the sundial or marked candle to the minutes and seconds of our quartz watches. Today, however, the measure of time is no longer just figures on a dial; it is also images displayed on the screens and monitors of 'real time'. The old pendulum movement and clockwork mechanisms, as well as the throbbing of quartz watches, are thus giving way to the movement of the shutter, as cameras and their monitors become so many 'precision watches' or model light-clocks.

The old chronometric system of before, during and after will thus probably be superseded by a 'chronoscopic' system of underexposed, exposed and overexposed.

In the time of succession, duration is paradoxically considered as a series of instants *without any duration*, after the manner of the geometric line conceived as a sequence of points without any dimension. But to this it is now necessary to oppose the concept of exposure time, which ultimately leads us to think of all the (physiological and technological) 'picture-taking' procedures as so many *intakes of time*.

This 'lighting up' of the relativist concept of temporality would lead us into a fundamental revision of the status of the different magnitudes of space and time, such that the light interval overrides the classical intervals of extension and duration. To the daylight of astronomical time should logically be added the daylight of technological speed: from the chemical daylight of candles through the electrical daylight of the Edison lamp (the same Edison who invented the kinetoscope) to the electronic daylight of computer terminals, that deceptive indirect light propagated at the speed of light waves, those transmitter-receivers and other visual generators of duration which still and moving photography and video-computer graphics represent alongside traditional timepieces.

* * *

This *indirect light* is ultimately the result of the fusion of optics and kinematics, a fusion which now embraces the whole range of ocular, graphic, photographic and cinematographic representations, making each of our images a kind of *shadow of time* – no longer the customary 'passing time' of historical linearity but the 'exposed time' which (as we said) surfaces. This is the time of Niepce's photographic developing, the time of the Lumière Brothers' cinematographic resolution of movement, but now above all *the time of videographic high definition* of a 'real-time' representation of appearances which cancels the very usefulness of passive (geometric) optics in favour of an active optics capable of causing the decline of the direct transparency of matter. What is inordinately privileged by this process is the indirect (electro-optical) transparency of light or – to be even more precise – of the light of the speed of light.

Thus, after the nuclear disintegration of the space of matter which led to the political situation we know today, the disintegration of *the time of light* is now upon us. Most likely, it will bring an equally major cultural shift in its wake, so that the depth of time will finally win out over the depth of spatial perspective inherited from the Renaissance.

* * *

'There is no longer any distance. You are so close to things that they no longer affect you at all,' wrote Joseph Roth in 1927.[3]

One can well imagine the importance this had for the planning of space: whereas it used to be just a question of arranging our environment to house our bodily activities, the point now is to *control* that environment through interactive online techniques.

In fact, there is an inversion of the classical architectural organization. Instead of various domestic functions being successively distributed around the space that is used for living, all the occupant's activities are concentrated at a single-point remote control so that he or she does not have to move about. 'Meeting at a distance', the paradox of home-based work, becomes through interactivity 'gathering at one point that which is kept at a distance'. Obviously the user occupying these absolute 'restrooms' is the one who constitutes this point, or centre, of inertia, and so they have nothing in common with the distribution of tasks in the traditional domestic set-up.

The individual's *centre of intensive time* therefore becomes the organizing centre of the home. The 'milieu' of the occupant's present time becomes the preponderant milieu of the habitat, to the detriment of any spatial concentration. Successive fragmentation suddenly gives way to the control of simultaneity, the emergence of a directing centre in the shape of a remote-control or even verbally controlled device, if the system is sufficiently developed to respond to his master's voice.

Rather as in the space environment described by Ludwig Boltzmann, where the living being's weightless present becomes the sole temporal referent replacing both future and past – and also, we should not forget, the sole inertial referent in the environment control of the intelligent home – the *self-referent* dominates all external references and the endogenous holds sway over the exogenous.

Some readily speak here of a strengthened individualism, but it really involves a transfer of the space-time of human residence, a transfer from the 'extensive' domain of external references (mass, area, climate, etc.) to the solitary intensive realm of the *self-reference of a being present here and now*. Instantaneous remote action upon the environment suddenly takes over from the customary action through communication.

'To inhabit energy' (heat, light, etc.) or 'to be inhabited by energy' then becomes a cruel dilemma for the user, but above all for the architect responsible for the synchronism or diachronism of the space and time of strictly human action.

'This house has become my own body and its horror – my own

heart,' cried the architect Varelli in Dario Argento's film *Inferno*. And indeed, if the real-time milieu of the user's *intensive present* definitively gains the upper hand over the milieu of real space, architecture suffers a disturbing regression. Where spatial depth used to play a part in rationally organizing the home from floor to ceiling (through the distribution of hallways, corridors and staircases), 'temporal depth' (of real-time immediacy and ubiquitousness) undermines and dissolves that rational organization. From the order of *succession*, we suddenly pass to the disorder of *simultaneity*. Here again, the time of succession gives way to the time of exposure. Even if the general volumetry of the building remains unchanged in order to house the occupant's body, it loses its ergonomic foundation, its organic relationship to action, necessary movement and distinctively human animation. For the practical efficiency of the intelligent home rests upon the *omnipresence* and *omnivoyance* of a resident who no longer even needs to be there to operate the various instruments, a telephone call being enough for his slightest wish to be met.

Here is the latest twittering of such home-based interactivity.

Thomson presents SECURISCAN, a computer-run system that can be remotely programmed and interrogated, a combination of comfort and security that allows automation and monitoring of the basic household chores as well as protection of home and person. An electronic exchange receives information coming in from the peripherals. The owner's remote-control device is accepted and his home welcomes him with a synthesized voice, but an intruder sets off alarms and warning lights while the exchange notifies the police.

This general exchange has built into it a household function manager which, in response to a simple telephone call, can switch on the heating, lighting or even the garden sprinkler. 'This standard model,' we learn from the publicity, 'can always have other functions added to it. In particular, since SECURISCAN detects breakdowns and major hazards (gas or water leaks, etc.), *it may also prove an excellent home-nurse*.'[4]

Finally, let us note that this mechanical domestic is cordless and operates at high frequencies.

If extension or distance is no longer a limit to power, present being is no longer so much here and now as *potential* – that is, 'potential' *in absolute speed*.

Here we find the insoluble problem facing the architect and town planner: namely the paradoxical *generalized* (real-time) arrival which now supersedes the limited (real-space) arrival of physical movement from one point to another.

In fact, while this type of movement is still evidently one constant in the volumetric arrangement of built space, the latter's customary necessity is more and more yielding to environment control pure and simple.

Already in the nineteenth century, the appearance of block lifts and escalators or moving walkways helped to *relativize* access to both height and area, as these prostheses complemented in fixed property what the railway, underground and motor car had achieved in the movable domain.

In this final part of the twentieth century, however, the situation is reversed: the famed new *mobility* of public and private transport is giving way to the *immobility* of transmission, to that home inertia which some already call 'cocooning'.

Just as Paul Morand's 'man in a hurry' could no longer invest in anything that took too long, so the man 'under stress' from the contemporary environment shuts himself away not just at home but *inside himself*. Like a motor-disabled person, the occupant of these *endogenous zones* concentrates on his ego not out of egoistic individualism but because of the cruelly demanding schema of temporality governing his action, or rather his interaction with a 'human milieu' that is no longer a place [*un lieu*], to the very extent that his main activity is temporal.[5]

* * *

A Polish architect who had been seriously injured in a traffic accident once explained to me that at the moment when the Warsaw bus hit his taxi he had a feeling of 'spherical projection'; the world seemed to rush upon him, in the manner of a 3-D film. As a magnet attracts metals, so did my friend's body suddenly attract the surrounding space of buildings, windows and cars – even the unhealthy curiosity of passers-by when he came round again.

To find oneself at the centre is always a trying experience. It is well known that to be the object of public attention and expectation causes a kind of fright and quickened heartbeat, and yet this is an exceptional situation which occurs only at rare moments in a lifetime. In environment control, however, the *stage* is there at every moment of one's life, all day and all night.

At the interactive centre of the 'home pilot' system, the occupant is rather like a car driver in the midst of heavy city traffic: reflex activity is more important than reasoning, and stress prolongs the moments when he is powerless to change things or to move forward – for example, when the traffic has slowed down or the road is blocked. The intelligent home presents the same kind of trials. Far from being the acme of domestic comfort, the new *domotics* involves a special kind of temporary or permanent disablement whose only parallel is the situation following a traffic accident, except that here the 'paralysis' is actually intended.

Already with the spread of electrification in the thirties, electric light produced curious reactions among people used to the oil lamp. A peasant woman once explained to me: 'The really funny thing when I flick the switch is that *the light comes on behind me.*' She had been used to lighting a lamp or candles and bringing the flame to the table or mantelpiece, so that for her the technical surprise of electricity was not the greater brightness but *the physical gesture of bringing light.*

What changes through electronic environment control, however, is not just one familiar gesture but the whole ergonomics of behaviour, with the possible exception of the acts of eating, washing, dressing or going to the toilet.

The only parallel to this sudden gestural rarefication is the katalavox, tetravox or other electronic prosthesis employing the paralytic's own voice, or similar devices used by F–16 or Mirage 2000 fighter pilots. (In fact, the able but *overequipped* air force pilot resembles in every feature the *equipped invalid*, the paraplegic or tetraplegic able to use some residual bodily function [a cheek or the tip of his tongue] to steer him around the home environment.)

The blind or paralysed person is now the model for the 'sight-disabled' or 'motor-disabled' occupant of the intelligent home.

If space is what prevents everything from being in the same place, domotics means that there is no longer any domestic space or stage, but only domestic time, a kind of usual temporality rarefied in the extreme.

Absolutely everything rushes at the occupant. The real-time interface (the remote control) dresses the user in interactive space in a kind of *data suit.* Instead of just having a few familiar portable objects such as a watch or a walkman, he is *invested with the power* to control his domestic environment.

Rather as an instrument panel shows how a vehicle's engine is performing, the user's energy and motor body triggers the reflex operation of the classical architectonic functions. However the rooms and spaces are arranged or distributed, the architectonic ensemble interacts with *the finger and eye*, sometimes just with the voice.

Here it is (electro-magnetic) speed which governs the architecture, as (electric) light illuminates its spaces. In the end, people are not so much *in* the architecture; it is more the architecture of the electronic system which invades them, which is *in* them, in their will to power, their reflexes, their least desires, every hour of the day and night.

How is it possible to live from day to day with such a chimera on one's back? How can one use such a potential *without collapsing into one's own ego*, just as astrophysicists promise for the solar system?

As a boomerang returns to its thrower, so does the intelligent home go back to its source in *present being*. The disorder of its passions, the brusqueness of its reflexes are all that organize the space-time of residence. When one knows the bad effects that zapping has on how films are constructed, it is not hard to imagine the damage done by environment control to architectonics. Similarly, when one observes the harm caused by raging drivers, one can imagine the secret dramas, the *parking accidents*, of the home automation of the future.

'Deconstruction' is, to be sure, the order of the day, but certainly not in the way that some contemporary architects think. *Deconstruction is the result of the new primacy of real time over space*, of instant interactivity over customary activity, and of the 'trans-appearance' described above over the very appearance of things.[6]

To control the environment, then, is not so much to furnish or inhabit it as to be *inhabited* or engulfed by the domestic organs that populate it. Rather as air conditioning succeeded the thermal comfort of walls, the whole of a building will tomorrow come as a package conditioned by domotics, the domotics that is merely the borrowed name of the deconstruction of the old domestic residence.

The 'tele-present' occupant of telematic restrooms is in the position of a miracle-worker. To the *omnivoyance* of the sudden trans-appearance of things is added another divine attribute, namely remote *omnipresence*, a kind of electro-magnetic telekinesis. Thus, the house is literally haunted by its occupant's spirit or will to power, as the occupant is in turn constantly preoccupied by his building.

As the power of his will supplants the old distances that had to be covered, and even the dimensions of the built space, the user of this immediate dwelling becomes the energetic director or motor of an environment that may just as easily be close as distant. There is a kind of *reciprocal bewitchment* here between the individual and the place that houses him, a bewitchment made possible simply through the feat of speed performed by a radio or video signal.

The example of Scott Fisher's virtual environment helmet is

particularly revealing of this dramatic change. In the 'portable simulator' (fashioned after a motorcycle helmet), a complete virtual environment featuring architectural volume, cockpit, control room, instrument panel, and so on, is reconstituted through computer technology, so that the wearer can take instant action by means of captors which equip his hands (the data glove), his feet, or indeed his whole body (the data suit). Thus, the man can take or move *virtual objects* with his *quite real hands*, thanks to a fictitious image of the surroundings that appears on his simulator helmet screen.

The situation is similar with our real environment control: the distances and times that usually separate various functions are abolished through the virtues of domotics. That which used to make up the very reality of space, and of the use of space, now vanishes. Human use no longer gives constructed space its characteristic quality, for *the remote-control device virtualizes measurable distance between things*. In order to 'realize' environment control of the interactive dwelling, it is necessary to 'derealize' classical architectonic space. Thus the difference becomes minute, less than minute, between the software-generated *virtual environment* where one acts with a body equipped with nerve impulse detectors, and the architect-produced *real environment* where one instantly acts over a distance by means of zapping or purely vocal commands.

Derealization of a simulated environment where one *really* acts will therefore go together with 'realization' of an actually built environment where one acts virtually by means of electro-magnetic waves.

For future missions to Mars, Fisher is also preparing a *robot technician* with the latest interactive technology. An earthling based at NASA headquarters will be equipped with a data suit and a helmet relaying live vision of the Martian surface; *he will then be able to remote-guide a vehicle several light-years away on the red planet.*

The robot's video-sight will certainly be his own, as will the hands steering the instrument about. And when it cautiously moves around on the burning soil of Mars, it will be the feet of its human remote-guide that allows it to do so.

Literally possessed by its operator, Scott Fisher's robot will be the *double* of the human technician working it at a distance. Humans will no more tread the soil of the distant planet than people on earth will actually have to walk around their intelligent home.

As action and remote action, presence and tele-presence, become so tightly entangled with each other, the intensity of mechanical transmission signals and the intensity of human nervous impulses also tend to merge into one, effacing not only sidereal (or terrestrial) space but even the spatial extension of the animal body. For *bodily energy* is transferred to the machine – or, to be more precise, loco-motion commands are transferred from one 'body' to another, from one machine to another, *without any contact at all with any surface*. The 'man–machine' interface eliminates all physical supports one after the other, thus achieving a constant *weightlessness* between individual and place. The famous 'real time' here helps to erase both real space and all the bodies it contains, to the dubious benefit of a total virtualization of lived space and time.

It should not be forgotten, however, that the drawback of this weightlessness is spatial and temporal disorientation, a sweeping deconstruction of the real environment. 'Above' and 'below' become equivalent like 'past' and 'future', the sudden reversibility putting the body back at the *centre* of the surrounding world.

We are thus heading towards a situation where the key feature will be control over ego-centric (introverted) space, not, as in the past, the arrangement of exo-centric (extroverted) space. As self-refer-ence supplants the classical reference of some 'horizon line', indi-viduals will no longer refer to anything other than their own weight-mass or polarity.

* * *

'Coma is a state in which relations with the outside world are lost,' explains Professor Lemaire, head of the intensive care unit at Henri-Mondor Hospital in Créteil. 'After three minutes without brain oxy-genation, irreversible lesions appear which may go as far as brain death. In other cases, only the higher functions of memory, speech and motivity are affected, but the vital functions are preserved. That is what is called a vegetative state.'

Domestic interactivity, involving a progressive loss of relations with the external environment, is thus technically *a form of coma*. But it is a 'coma' that does not end in brain death and all the associ-ated ethical problems; it only leads to the 'vegetative state' of home inertia, a 'habitable coma' that is the exact opposite of the 'habitable circulation' of the traditional block of flats.

Already in the late seventies, the American craze for the sensory deprivation box and the all too famous *camera silenta* of German prisons heralded this blind-pulling on the body of the individual.

Some held the view that this illustrated the coming of a police state or the rise of individualism, but it pointed more to a shift in personal time away from the extensiveness of immediate action to the intensiveness of sensations, where certain delinquent or pathological situations prefigured the generalization of such behaviour.

'They don't want to die, they want to be dead,' a British psychiatrist explained at the time.

Today the situation has evolved still further and given rise to even more disturbing symptomatic reactions. 'We wanted to live intensely as long as possible, knowing that death was the only possible outcome,' Norbert Tallet's girl-friend stated to the examining magistrate of Libourne in January 1989, after she and Tallet had committed a long series of more or less gratuitous attacks.

This transfer – or, to be more precise, this *transfer accident* – from extensive personal time to intensive personal time illustrates the new and last figure of death: no longer the big sleep or disappearance, but the full blossoming of the individual's powers. Rather as the 'rising to extremes' characterizes mass warfare in Clausewitz's theory, so does 'rising power' now characterize civil peace in a mass society where *instant switching* (and drugs) wreak such havoc.

This sudden shift in personal time is imperceptibly leading our species towards dramatic destruction of the physical environment, but also towards a deconstruction of domestic space in which the tempting myth of 'absolute shelter' will soon be a tangible reality. Not only will there be no need to *go out* to work, have fun or do the shopping, but it will be unnecessary to *go in*, since the intelligent home will have no opening, no entrance door. Instead, a kind of hood will cover the locomotive body, as the barrel of a sarcophagus or the cell of a cabin houses, or rather covers, the body of a mummy or pilot equally well.

Environment control, whether close or distant, is thus leading our societies towards a final technological hybrid whose ergonomic archetype is the seat or 'throne' capable of turning itself into a bed, an invalid's litter.

In the extra-vehicular activities of the American space shuttle, we can see the same shift in the centre of gravity: from the astronaut's body to a jet-propelled seat that replaces man's natural motivity as soon as he leaves the spaceship to move around in weightlessness.

With the primacy accorded to the 'real time' of interactivity over the real space of customary activity, are we moving towards home activity on earth analogous to the activity of astronauts moving around in high orbit? Unfortunately, this probably is the case, since the *general inrush* of data and images is finally placing us in the same position of inertia – a domestic inertia that radically alters our relationship to the world, our relations with the *real* (terrestrial or extra-terrestrial) environment.

We should be in no doubt: whereas *limited inflows* used to require some upward physical movement in the act of rising and going out, or movement from near to far in the act of travelling, the decline of such activity represents for the human species a shift as great as that involved in the passage to an *upright gait*. The difference is that there is no longer 'positive evolution' to a new type of motivity, but, rather, 'negative behavioural involution' leading towards a pathological fixedness: the coming of *seated man* or, worse still, *couched man*.

Notes

1. Maurice Merleau-Ponty, *L'Oeil et l'esprit*, Paris: Gallimard, p. 78.
2. See the final chapter of Paul Virilio, *The Vision Machine*, London: British Film Institute, 1994.
3. *Die Flucht ohne Ende*, Munich 1978.
4. Quoted [and retranslated] from sales publicity issued in 1989.
5. Paul Klee.
6. See Paul Virilio, *The Lost Dimension*, New York: Semiotext(e), 1991.

5

POLAR INERTIA

Stop the earth: I'm getting off.

Jean Laude

Is there a privileged here? Yes, absolute kinaesthetic zero: the *zero of energy*, wrote Husserl in notes composed in the thirties.

Kinaesthetic space is thus a system of possible places as *stopping point*, as beginning and end of calm.

> This primary world which is constituted in stationary kinaesthetic activity, in the inaction of 'walking kinaesthetics', is a world which is firmly oriented about my physical animate organism (or the null-point constituted in it). If walking begins, all worldly things therefore continue to appear to me to be oriented about my phenomenally stationary, resting organism. That is, they are oriented with respect to here and there, left and right, etc., *whereby a firm zero of orientation persists, so to speak, as absolute here.*[1]

In a footnote written at the same time, however, Husserl ponders this 'absolute zero' of movement: 'The prone position, being the most comfortable, ought to be the *zero position*. So it must be taken into consideration that the normal zero is a problem'[2] – which is the least that can be said! This premonitory work, one of the last written by the German phenomenologist, illustrates the sharp break which occurred at that time between physics and philosophy. From the geocentrism of Antiquity to Husserl's ego-centrism, there is a clear shift: from the earth as centre (the axis of reference for the Ancients) to this *living present* as centre, of which Ludwig Boltzmann said as early as 1897 that it was absolute self-reference.

Just as the 'world-assailing technologies' (Heidegger) were about to develop, the old master declared his hostility to everything that the upheaval represented. Husserl's famous 'European crisis' was never anything but a wise man's distress signal in the face of that machine of total mobilization for whose coming Ernst Jünger so fervently prayed.

What are we to make today of this phenomenological point of view on the basic fixation: *the world as proto-foundation of meaning*?[3]

Strangely enough, the philosopher's intuition is becoming topical again, with the important difference that the 'polar inertia' described here is not so much original as terminal.

For at the dawn of total war, the known world was still a solitary world, the single *mundus* of human experience. The 'zero point' designated by Husserl is not at all different from the *axis mundi* of Galileo's time, and it was necessary to wait another thirty-five years – until the moon landing of 21 July 1969, to be precise – for the reference ground [*sol*] to lose its importance and to become an *entresol*.[4]

Here again is Husserl: 'In conformity with its original idea, the earth does not move and does not rest; only in relation to it are motion and rest given as having their sense of motion and rest.'[5] And further on:

As long as I do not have a presentation of a new basis, as a basis, from which the earth can have sense in interconnected and returning locomotion as a self-contained body in motion and at rest, and as long as an exchange of bases is not presented such that both bases become bodies, to that extent just the earth itself is the basis and not a body. *The earth does not move.*[6]

Now, this is precisely what the logistics of total mobilization would 'revolutionize', in the Copernican sense of the term. The effort to develop German rockets at Peenemünde would end in liquidation of the ground of reference, when the *axis mundi* lost for ever its absolute value. 'Zero altitude': those words uttered by the pilot at the end of Apollo 11's landing manoeuvres on the moon indicated that, at that precise moment, altitude had become 'distance' pure and simple, that there was now another ground or basis, a *ground up above*. In the course of that summer, in 1969, looking at the moon became the same as looking at an island from a shoreline. The obliterated sky, the landing of humans on another planet, gave us a balcony view of the void. The outer limits suddenly became a starry coast.

But this sudden importance of the limits was itself comparable to a disappropriation, as the celestial object called earth was henceforth of less interest than the time and space separating the two heavenly bodies. In fact, this great change broke up both an order of representing the world and an order of utilization. The event was not so much the transmission of television pictures to earth over a distance of more than 300,000 kilometres, as the *simultaneous view of the moon on the TV screen and through the window*.[7]

On that day, Husserl's desperate attempt to 'invert the Copernican doctrine' found fulfilment. As the cosmologist Stephen Hawking explained much later, science has become so technical that philosophers have been incapable of understanding it and theologians do not understand enough to contradict it. They no longer want to place themselves in the position that the Church adopted in Galileo's time.[8]

This is how things are in 1989, the twentieth anniversary of the moon landing as well as the year of the first translation into French of Husserl's text from the Louvain archives. But we should not forget how topical is this phenomenological research into the origins of the corporeality and spatiality of Nature, first of all with regard to the *ego-centredness* of individual being. The fact that the original ground or basis has lost its status as 'absolute ground' has the awesome consequence of referring this phenomenological centredness to one's 'own body', the corporeality of the *living present* of which Ludwig Boltzmann spoke in his letter to Zermelo.

'I am not in motion. Whether I stay still or walk about, *my flesh is the centre* and the still and moving bodies are all around me, and I have a ground without mobility.' Even if the cadence of Husserl's sentence now strikes us as rather lame, the earlier words grow ever more forceful: the loss of territorial exo-centricity is increasing man's behavioural ego-centricity, not only 'in the void' but here below on earth, where the archetype of all bodily spatiality is becoming a lost ark of the experience of movement. This is the *decentring* which is a deconstruction not only of territorial and architectural planning but of the very environment of human experience.

This is the supreme egoism, an ego-centrism stronger than all the anthropocentrisms and geocentrisms that used to fashion history and geography and from which Copernicus, Galileo and Kepler tried to rescue us. Once the Creator has been eliminated as First Cause, where should the phenomenological reference, the absolute singularity, be placed if not at the end of the tunnel of astrophysics, at the Big Bang – or else deep down in the 'living present' that is the measure of all things for Boltzmann, Husserl and a number of others?

The German philosopher warns us that his is an immoderate enterprise. But we should not forget that this immoderateness corresponds to that of the technicized science which appeared at the dawn of total war.

> One may find that it is wrong to rather extravagantly contradict all natural-scientific knowledge [. . .]. But even if one found in our attempts the most unbelievable philosophical hubris – we would not back down from the consequences for the clarification of necessities pertaining to all bestowal of sense *for what exists and for the world*.[9]

Further on, regarding the legitimation of this science without consciousness, Husserl writes:

> We confront [here] the great problem of the correct sense of a universal, purely physical science of 'Nature' – of an astronomical-physical science operating in 'astronomical' infinity in the sense of our modern physics (in the broadest sense, astrophysics), and the problem of an inner infinity, the infinity of the continuum and the way to atomize or quantify – atomic physics – in the open endlessness or infinity. In these sciences of the infinity of the totality of Nature, the mode of observation is usually the one in which animate organisms are only accidentally particularized bodies which can therefore also conceivably be completely ignored so that a Nature without organisms, without brutes and humans, is possible.[10]

This, we should remember, was written in 1934. A few years later, there would be Auschwitz then Hiroshima and Nagasaki, and much later, the landing on the moon thanks to fall-out from the universal science denounced by the old master.

* * *

Once lunar soil is reached, the loss of extension, the forfeiture of Husserl's alma mater, brings with it the decline of that constituted world-time which he sees as indistinguishable from psychological time: 'The ego lives and precedes all actual and possible beings [. . .]. *Constituted world-time conceals in itself psychological time.*'[11]

To lose one's foothold is thus also to lose or waste one's time, or at least to lose the relationship of the time of a diminished world to the constitutive time of psychology. Loss of the reference ground brings an equally major decline in *reference time*, as Boltzmann expressed it so well.

The bodily ego-centricity which today survives the loss of the original ark (an ark called 'earth' since the acquisition of a *ground up above*) goes hand in hand with a temporal ego-centricity in which psychological time definitively wins out over the time of the constituted world.

For the convinced phenomenologist, then, the loss of 'terrestrial distance' is not so much due to the power of transmitters to nullify extension in the perceptible world; it mainly results from *the new dominance of psychological time*. The relativity of the living (of the living-present) is mixed in with the relativity of those technological vectors which complete the defeat of the constituted world, the decentring of animate being.

As a child grows older, everything that used to seem huge and disproportionate comes to look smaller and suddenly within reach. Alas, it is the same with expanses of land that keep shrinking until they are no longer there. Despite the promises of ecology, the earth will soon have exhausted all its resources, including its earliest vocation as a yardstick for human activities.

Speed really is the old age of the world, of this world of bodily and spatial experience, of an earth – or, rather, a ground – which is becoming fragile in the extreme, as in an irreversible atrophy due to organic senility.

As they shrivel more and more, the seas and mountains are polluted not so much by toxic waste as by what Husserl already denounced as the noxious technology bound up with a supposedly catholic, universal science. It is a science which snuffs out all exotic references one by one, all our *external reverences* (including to any 'creator'), to the benefit of an absolute singularity – another name for the *accident of accidents*, the birth of time. This ubiquitous desire to observe – to *see live*, why not? – the production of a primal time expresses better than any philosophical discourse on the 'invention' of time the will to power of universal science.[12] It is less a question of contemplating Genesis, as a passive observer, than of assessing, as an active competitor, how to control and manipulate time as was done not long ago with the physical extension of matter or the intensity of light. Finally to achieve the demiurge's dream of dreams: to create an ersatz time in which there is no passing of time, to manufacture a scheme of temporality that escapes the usual constraints!

'Starting from zero, we have a directional beam in which, however, the problem of the normal "zero" position still has to be clarified.'[13] This sentence of Husserl's concerning the individual's position in the world has since shifted its place under the impact of astrophysics: from the centre of the ego to the centre of the 'zero time' of cosmology. The questions once posed by the phenomenologist, the metaphysician, are now posed for the physicist and the astrophysicist.

'How was the first minute of the universe? The intensity of timeless time, of zero time?' – since the Second World War these questions have supplanted the customary philosophical question: 'What is the consciousness of the instant, the intensity of being-now?'

This shift reveals the undoing of philosophy. As a logistics expert indicated at the beginning of the century in connection with military movements: 'The more mobility increases, the greater is the control.' And indeed, the more the speed of movement increases, the more control becomes absolute, omnipresent. The more speed grows, the more 'control' tends to supplant the environment itself, so that the real time of interactivity finally replaces the real space of bodily activity.

Speed thus really is the old age of man's real environment, the premature ageing of that world constituted by and constitutive of the objective reality of which Husserl used to speak – a final ageing not only of the 'primal' towns and countryside, but also of the whole ecological expanse commonly known as 'earth' or, if you like, of its original soil or ground.

What we are witnessing is the progressive disappearance of the space of anthropological-geographic reference in favour of a mere *visual piloting*, central control of the ceaseless 'transfers of responsibility' that will soon have created a new horizon of human experience. The sentence by Werner von Braun quoted as an epigraph above – 'Tomorrow, to learn space will be as useful as learning to drive a car' – perfectly illustrates this process.

One correction is needed, however, since the space evoked by the technician from Peenemünde is no longer the 'full space' of the primal ark but the *empty space* of an extra-terrestrial vessel, the final ark which is coming to replace the 'space-time' of our ordinary experience of place with that of the non-place of the 'space-speed' of technology.

Thus, speed really is the 'transfer accident', the premature ageing of the constituted world. Carried away by its extreme violence, we do not go anywhere; we merely abandon the *living* in favour of the *void* of rapidity. As a racing driver must first master acceleration, keep his car straight and pay no heed to the details of the surrounding space, so too will it doubtless be for every human activity, both at and away from home. We will no longer admire the landscape but only watch our screens and monitor our interactive trajectory – that is, a 'journey' with no distance, a 'travelling time' with no actual passing of time.

Everything that has previously been involved in the arrangement of real urban and rural space will tomorrow simply be a matter of organizing the real-time conductivity of images and information.

To divide up real space, to control the environment, has been the avowed aim of all geopolitics right from the origins of the city-state and feudal land grids up to the completion of the nation-state. Tomorrow, environment control will help to achieve a veritable 'chrono-politics', nay, a *dromo-politics*, in which the nation will give way to social deregulation and transpolitical deconstruction. Remote control will gradually replace not only direct command but above all ethics (the Ten Commandments), as those famous 'ethics committees' already portend in the field of genetics and soon, no doubt, in various ecological, economic or strategic areas.

* * *

Against a background of atmospheric pollution and ozone holes, another hole has recently developed in the earth. *Our planet is slipping away*: not as a cosmic express moving at thirty kilometres per second, but as a rapidly deflating toy balloon. Since we are always being told that distances are shrinking and the earth becoming smaller, it would seem an urgent matter to draw the consequences!

On the threshold of the sixties General Chassin declared: 'Military people have never taken account of the fact that the earth is round.' And what about 'civilians'? But still, this is not a good formulation. The problem is less the roundness of the planet than the fact that estimates of area will soon be a thing of past, that the geophysical environment will be devalued for ever.

Can one even imagine losing the space and time that constitute the body's axis of reference? Can one seriously think that we will become oblivious to place, to all places? Or that behavioural ego-centricity will become the only polarity of the individual, not so much 'in the world' as in himself? Yet those who find this difficult fail to notice that many of us are already training for it here and there, in business, the arts or war. Listen, for example, to the designer Alessandro Mendini:

> Man is himself a set of instruments. If I sit on the ground, I am a seat. If I walk, I am a means of transport. If I sing, I am a musical instrument. The body is the primary set of objects at man's disposal, whereas tools are its artificial extensions, its monstrous prostheses. The primitive man, the nomad, the hitch-hiker condense their tools in themselves – they coincide with their own home. *They are a house, an architecture.*

This has all been known since Leroy-Gourhan, of course, but the question is always wrongly posed since what is concentrated in us is not only 'instruments' but the *environment*. What coincides with us in real time, therefore, is no longer some house or architecture but the *oikumen*, the whole of the inhabited earth. 'I have been everything and everything is nothing,' said the Stoic Marcus Aurelius. Should we now say: 'I am the earth, I am the man-planet'? It is obviously hard to accept, but it is nevertheless the case.

Should we think that the 'program trading' or automatic quoting of stock values in the City of London and Wall Street, commonly referred to as the 'Big Bang', affects only the global economy? What a mistake! The implosion of real time now conditions all exchanges, and the computer-driven crash of 1987 was but an advance sign of other economic catastrophes, and above all of dramatic breaks in the field of trade and social communication. In fact, the faster information circulates, the more the control of all exchange increases and tends to become absolute. *Omnipresence is meant to make such control the substitute for man's environment, his earth, his only milieu.*

Everything that was acted out in dividing the territory is now acted out not only, as before, in organizing the social body, but in controlling the animal body of this human being, less 'in the world' than *within himself*. Hence the fragility of human 'self-consciousness', which has been more invaded by technologies than invested with new responsibilities.

The egotism of individuals rendered almost inert by the interactive capacities of their milieu has nothing in common with any philosophical 'personalism'. Rather, it recalls the infirmity of those who are described as suffering from 'multiple handicaps'.

When a young media figure was recently asked what really filled him with dread, he replied: 'The idea that everything might become static, that the machine might grind to a halt. That's why I never take more than ten days' holiday. I'm terrified of immobility.' This foreboding, worthy of a driver afraid of running out of petrol, reveals the hypertension of people living today. Everybody can easily imagine the standstill that will certainly affect them one day or another, not only the sclerosis due to old age and loss of reflexes, but a behavioural inertia due to speed and the reduced depth of field of their immediate activities.

Unless . . . unless they fully accept the inevitability of that corpse-like fixity, in the manner of Howard Hughes, the bedridden client of Desert Inn in Las Vegas. With its architectural mix of airframe and staging post, today's hotel room illustrates better than any other domestic environment the way in which the human habitat has evolved. No longer is there a 'reception' desk, only a machine that communicates with your credit card; no longer a hotelkeeper, only an access code that is automatically cancelled after twenty-four hours; no more rooms, but 'boxes' nine or even six square metres in dimension; no more chambermaids, but cleaning companies. Sometimes, as in the Cocoon chain hotel near Roissy airport, the cells do not even have any windows but only an internal system of air conditioning. The model here is obviously the parking lot, a place to 'park' human beings little different from their accompanying luggage.

* * *

Evidence is the reason why questioning has been neglected. That things should be evident from the very start has become a postulate. (Husserl)

Indeed, if the relativity of the visible has become self-evident, it is because the evidence of the implicit has already superseded that of the explicit. No longer to believe your eyes has become an inevitability, so that loss of faith in perception develops *ad infinitum* the loss of religious faith begun in the Age of Enlightenment. If God is dead, as Nietzsche claimed, it is because the omnipotence of the look (*theos*) has been extinguished for ever. The *absolute* look of the divine (creator) and the *relative* look of the human (observer): both have been dragged into the fall of definitive blindness.

When ecology suddenly emerged in the United States in the sixties, significantly at the same time as the moon landing, it appeared as *the science of a world for ever lost as a human milieu*, a privileged and unlimited *mundus* of the human individual. Exhausted and threatened on all sides, our planet is already no more than a residue, a 'reserve' to be preserved with the utmost urgency. But the so-called environmental revolution never did more than point to a world that had had its day as the biosphere of the species. What appears in its place is not so much an industrial 'technosphere' as a 'dromosphere' that eradicates the human continuum, as Husserl warned on the eve of the general mobilization.

Today some physicists, like Stephen Hawking, who holds Newton's chair as Lucasian Professor of Mathematics at Cambridge University, still tell us that when we combine quantum mechanics with general relativity, it is possible *for both space and time to form together a finite, four-dimensional space*, without singularity and without boundaries, *like the earth's surface* but with more dimensions.[14] But in transferring to the whole universe the model of the lost globe, of the terrestrial sphere closed on itself, this once again expresses the old geocentrism of astronomy.

Here again is Hawking: 'One could say: "The boundary condition of the universe is that it has no boundary." The universe would be completely self-contained and not affected by anything outside itself.

It would neither be created nor destroyed. *It would just BE.*'[15] The transference is perfectly clear: the universe is Yahweh, God, *He Who Is.* Disturbed at the possibility of cosmological fixism, however, Hawking writes:

> [I]t is possible for space-time to be finite in extent and yet to have no singularities that formed a boundary or edge. Space-time would be like the surface of the earth, only with two more dimensions. The surface of the earth is finite in extent but it doesn't have a boundary or edge: if you sail off into the sunset, you don't fall off the edge or run into a singularity. (I know, because I have been round the world!)[16]

If Hawking is to be believed, the only difference in nature between the astronomy of the Ancients and his own is the question of dimensions – or, in other words, the nature of measure. For the physicist in the end, *God is dimension* or, more precisely, *dimension is God.*

The universe is finite, to be sure, but it is 'without edges'. For Hawking everything is in this purely topological paradox. Let us look closely at what he says.

> Under the no boundary proposal one learns that the chance of the universe being found to be following most of the possible histories is negligible, but there is a particular family of histories that are much more probable than the others. *These histories may be pictured as being like the surface of the earth*, with the distance from the North Pole representing imaginary time and the size of a circle of constant distance from the North Pole representing the spatial size of the universe. The universe starts at the North Pole as a single point. As one moves south, the circles of latitude at constant distance from the North Pole get bigger, *corresponding to the universe expanding with imaginary time.* The universe would reach a maximum size at the equator and would contract with increasing imaginary time to a single point at the South Pole. Even though the universe would have zero size at the North and South Poles, these points would not be singularities, any more than the North and South Poles on the earth are singular.[17]

Thus, whereas for the philosopher Husserl the earth does not move, for the physicist Hawking it *swells* or *fills out*: it tries to get bigger than the ox in the fable.

As to the crucial question of the arrow of astrophysical time:

> The history of the universe in *real time*, however, would look very different. At about ten or twenty thousand million years ago, it would have a minimum size, which was equal to the maximum radius of the history in imaginary time. At later real times, the universe would expand like the chaotic inflationary model proposed by Linde [. . .]. The universe would expand to a very large size and eventually it would collapse again into what looks like a singularity in real time. [. . .] *Only if we could picture the universe in terms of imaginary time would there be no singularities.*[18]

And a little later, Hawking argues that when we return to the real time in which we live, some further singularities appear which might mean that what we call 'imaginary time' is in fact 'real time', and what we call 'real time' is but a figment of our imagination.

Here we find the same doubling as in other fields: real time and imaginary time for the astrophysicist, real time and recorded time for the electronic specialist in instant telecommunication. In both cases, the traditional threesome of past, present and future increasingly loses its usefulness.

On page 143 of *A Brief History of Time*, Hawking explains why this is so: 'When one tried to unify gravity with quantum mechanics, one had to introduce the idea of "imaginary" time. *Imaginary time is indistinguishable from directions in space.*' The sphere, then, is no longer the *terra firma* of Husserl's 'full world', but only the sphere of the 'histories' or 'trajectories' of an *empty* world, a world voided of substance.

'Imaginary' time is no less so than the space described here, as pure *direction*, pure *dimension*. Besides, when the cosmologist declares that what we call 'imaginary time' is perhaps only real time, and that what we call 'real time' is never more than a figment of our imagination, he reflects the present uncertainty about the *reality* principle of the concepts of space and time: not so much the spatio-temporal unity of a (Einsteinian) continuum as the reversibility of one or the other term, as soon as the heretical concepts of imaginary time and virtual speed are accepted for the 'histories' or trajectories that give form to the cosmos.

* * *

The question of Ancient philosophers: 'Does the earth move or does it remain the axis or hub of cosmic reality?' has thus recently given way to the question of the 'arrow of time' and the presence or absence of an original singularity called the Big Bang.

The analogy with pre-Copernican fixity is apparent enough, but with the difference that the beginning of time prevails over the beginning of space, and that the ideal sphere is no longer the terrestrial globe but a *virtual sphere* that swells and fills out in all directions (according to all possible trajectories), whereas the *real sphere* of the full world deflates and shrinks most lamentably, losing its substantive value along with its dimensions.

It is here that ecology reaches the limits of its theoretical narrowness, for it lacks a way of tackling the temporality schemas associated with ecosystems, especially those stemming from the industrial tech-nosphere. As a science of the finite world, the science of the ter-restrial environment seems deliberately to deprive itself of its relationship to 'psychological time'. After the fashion of that uni-versal science denounced by Husserl, ecology does not really address the 'man/machine' dialogue, the close interdependence of the various schemes of perception and human practices. In short, the discipline of ecology does not sufficiently echo the impact of Machine Time on the environment but leaves this concern to ergonomics or even politics.

Always this disastrous lack of understanding of the relativist char-acter of human activities (industrial and post-industrial)! It is here that *dromology* now comes into the picture. For unless 'ecology' is conceived as the political profit-and-loss administration of the sub-stances making up the geophysical environment, it can no longer develop without apprehending the 'economy of time' (or, more pre-cisely, space-time) of human activities and their rapid mutations. If, according to Charles Péguy, 'there is no history but only the passing of *public time*', then the very rhythm and speed of world events should give rise not only to a 'true sociology', as the poet suggests, but above all to a genuine *public dromology*. For we should never forget that the truth of phenomena is always limited by the speed at which they spring up.

To appreciate the scale of the current changes regarding the environment, or 'public space', let us consider what Marvin Minsky (founder of the MIT artificial intelligence laboratory) wrote in 1981:

> You put on a comfortable jacket lined with captors and motors functioning as muscles, and each movement of your arm, hand and fingers is reproduced *at a different place* by mobile mechanical hands. Light, clever and strong, these hands have their own captors through which you see and feel what is happening. Thanks to this instrument, you can 'work' in another room, another city, another country or another planet. Your remote representative has the strength of a giant or the delicacy of a surgeon.

Minsky confirms that this 'remote presence' is not a fiction: 'If we start acting consistently from now on, we might have *a remote-controlled economy* in the 21st century.' A few years later the Wall Street and London stock exchanges were setting up *program trading*, with the results that we know. And just a few months later, Scott Fisher was perfecting 'data gloves' and beginning to design 'data suits', both so close to Marvin Minsky's original intuition.

Let us now look at how this 'living-present' so dear to Ludwig Boltzmann changed its nature, so that nearly a century later it has

become a *tele-living-present*. At the end of his notes on the constitution of space, Edmund Husserl already wrote:

> If optical flesh functions in the optical field in any perception of a body, if kinaes-
> thesis is thus 'naturalized' in the quasi-bodily organ (the eye), how is this to be
> described? *Does not optical flesh, qua body, then have its place in the space of
> bodies*, as well as the property of being unable to go further in space, in a direc-
> tion where another body blocks its way? The following law prevails here: *a body
> cannot be where another body is*; they cannot pass through each other; they cannot
> be at rest in the same place.[19]

This statement, though now clearly superseded, does half-open the
question of the necessity of a reconstitution of real space, given the
premises of (real-time) interactivity and the 'presence' of persons
and things, however great the distance separating them.

For if man's sphere of activity is no longer limited by extension or
duration or even the opaqueness of obstacles barring his way, where
is his presence in the world, his real presence, actually located? 'Tele-
presence', no doubt, but where? From what starting point or position? Living-present, here and there at the same time, *where am I if
I am everywhere*?

My 'presence' then becomes as random as that of those phantom
particles whose position or speed may perhaps be known, but never
both at once. The indeterminacy principle thus now applies to the
reality of the 'subject' of experience as well as to its 'object'. The
question of *proprioception* has become central again.

At the end of an earlier work, I wrote: 'It is hard to imagine a
society that denied the body in the way that the soul has been more
and more denied – and yet, that is what we are heading towards.'[20]

Today this difficulty seems to have been partly resolved by the new
interactive technologies. Closer to what is far away than to what is
just beside us, we are becoming progessively detached from ourselves. Not only is the 'full body' of the earth vanishing before our
eyes, but our own body is also becoming blurred and afflicting us with
an unprecedented 'disorder', a paralysis (or autism) which leaves us
still *where we were*, with an imposing ponderous mass, while the loss
of the full body of being is carrying us towards the void. This 'void',
moreover, has nothing in common with the gap to be found in 'real'
space, since it is the void of a *virtual* environment, of a space-time
whose techniques of telecommunication are at once the beginning
and the end.

If vehicular technologies (balloon, aeroplane, rocket) progressively lifted us clear of the full body of the earth as the main reference for all human motion, until it was finally lost to us with the moon

landing twenty years ago, the *extra-vehicular* technologies of instant interactivity are now exiling us from ourselves and making us lose the ultimate physiological reference: that is, the ponderous mass of the locomotive body, the axis – or, to be more precise, the seat – of behavioural motivity and identity.

* * *

'*I am acted by an actor. He is inside my eyes; he touches with my hands*' – thus spoke the single character of *La Tragédie comique*, performed at the Bouffes du Nord theatre in the spring of 1989. At that one-man show, the actor Yves Hunstad wonderfully illustrated the paradox of a remote presence that makes it possible to avoid the opaque obstacle of a partner, rather in the way that Marvin Minsky foresaw eight years before.

The actor's paradox is thus turned inside out like a glove (a data glove). The character is no longer in search of an author, but rather of an *actor* upon whom to feed totally parasitically. Perched up on the moon, looking down to earth for an actor who can be 'acted', the 'character' tells an innocent child that he will be his 'actor'. What happens next can easily be imagined, especially as the character never stops inviting us to do the same.

Virtual environment, virtual presence, imaginary time: the parallel with interactive technologies is highly instructive, as if those technologies, having come from the 'theatre' of war, constantly returned to it through the development of civilian remote control and tele-surveillance. But here is what Yves Hunstad has to say of his profession: 'The actor, ever switching between life-roles, has a *fragile personality*; he throws himself body and soul into a different skeleton, a different brain. This allows him to go further, to be more audacious.'

When he said 'going further', he meant not in space off stage but *inside himself* on stage – to advance while remaining fixed to some theatrical or urban stage. A remote tele-presence would make it possible to escape the uniqueness of the living-present and to become anyone, anything, anywhere, microscope or telescope, a phenomenon of active, or rather *acting*, optics which thus answered in the affirmative Husserl's question: 'Does not optical flesh, qua body, have its place in the space of bodies?'

We should not forget, however, that this fable was entitled *La Tragédie comique*, a confusion of the tragic and the comic for a solitary individual who had become fragile in the extreme, an optical-flesh actor, and for anyone looking with minimal attention at the wretched substitution miracle of the theatrical or interactive stage. A theatrical production, being an urban phenomenon rooted in sedentariness, has always had as its first aim to prevent the audience from moving. The magnificence of the theatres and amphitheatres of Antiquity ultimately reflected *the invention of the very first stationary vehicle*, the pathological fixation of a populace upon the spectacle of the moving actor's optical flesh.

In fact, our 'civilization' has never known how to do anything other than keep extending the original urban sedentariness – from the Roman *insula* block of flats to the automotive furniture of the various 'means of transport' in modern Europe. The latest technologies of home interactivity and tele-presence will carry this process further still, thanks to the development of a final 'stationary vehicle' *to fix for ever* the personality of an individual (or, rather, a subject) whose only movement will be that of *the actor on a stage*. This tele-actor will no longer throw himself into any means of physical travel, but only into another body, an optical body; and he will go forward without moving, see with other eyes, touch with other hands than his own, to be over there without really being there, a stranger to himself, a deserter from his own body, an exile for evermore.

In the end, the ancient theatre will have been to the audiovisuality of the actor's optical flesh what the stadium already was to the automotivity of the athlete's physical body: that is, it will have invented motion *on the spot* instead of motion *in space*. In the eyes of people watching from the tiers, the actors will move their 'character' only within the narrow confines of the stage – a 'stage' which itself takes into account the orbital limits of the human gaze, only later, much later, introducing the online terminal that displays the space of an exotic and distant reality, after the fashion of a trip without travel such as only the theatre used to permit, thanks to the subjugation of both actor and spectator, and above all of the *character* and his *actor*, as Yves Hunstad so well illustrates.

After television, we shall see tele-action and tele-presence revive the possession of the body by an image, a mental image. This is the old myth of a doubling, not only of the actor's fragile personality but of the very reality of the external world, for a 'tele-actor' acting instantaneously in a geographical environment that has itself become virtual. The philosophical question is no longer who I really am but where I presently am.

This fusion of the ethical and the aesthetic, the endotic and the exotic, will bring about an ultimate inertia. No longer content to ask about his position or even his vitality, after the fashion of the particle mentioned by Heisenberg, the tele-acting individual would thus become *at the same time* (which is precisely 'real time') *uncertain* about his position in space and *indeterminate* with regard to his genuine schema of temporality. For the ponderous endo-reference of the physical body would suddenly give way to the behavioural exo-reference of an 'optical body', due only to the transmission speed of both vision and action.

In these conditions, how can one fail to see the role of the *last vehicle*, whose non-travelling traveller, non-passing passenger, would be the ultimate stranger, a deserter from himself, an exile both from the external world (the real space of vanishing geophysical extension) and from the internal world, alien to his animal body, whose mass would be as fragile as the body of the planet already is as it undergoes advanced extermination?

A recent feat will serve to illustrate this last assertion. In December 1986, for the first time in history, an aeroplane succeeded in circling the earth *without a stop*. Voyager – that was its name – thus erased the difference in kind between a low-orbiting satellite and a round-the-world aircraft. An object piloted by human hand escaped the ground as its basic reference.

Devised by the pilot's own brother, the engineer Burt Rutan, this orbiting aircraft prototype is but a first step in a much more ambitious project: namely, to create a flying machine driven by human energy alone (like the Gossamer Albatross of the engineer MacReady) and *capable of satellitizing a man by his own powers*; to make man not just the eagle's peer but the perfect equal of a star or asteroid. Man's own powers will then have achieved a state of inertia where his own bodily mass is identical to that of a weightless planet.

Notes

1. 'The World of the Living Present', in Edmund Husserl, *Shorter Works*, edited by P. McCormick and F.A. Elliston, University of Notre Dame Press, 1981, pp. 249–50. Emphasis added.

2. 'Notizen zur Raumkonstitution', *Philosophy and Phenomenological Research*, vol. 1, 1940–1, p. 30n.

3. See Edmund Husserl, 'The Origin of Geometry', in *Shorter Works*, pp. 255–70.

4. See Paul Virilio, *L'Insécurité du territoire*, Paris: Stock, 1976, pp. 93ff.

5. 'Foundational Investigations of the Phenomenological Origin of the Spatiality of Nature' [being an earlier part of the same manuscript as 'Notizen zur Raumkonstitution'], in *Shorter Works*, p. 223.

6. Ibid., p. 225. Emphasis added.

7. See *L'Insécurité du territoire*.

8. Stephen W. Hawking, *A Brief History of Time*, London: Bantam Press, 1990, p. 116.

9. 'Notizen zur Raumkonstitution', pp. 230–1. Emphasis added.

10. Ibid., p. 228.

11. Ibid., p. 231.

12. See Steven Weinberg, *The First Three Minutes: A Modern View of the Origin of the Universe*, London: Fontana, 1983.

13. 'Notizen zur Raumkonstitution', p. 30.

14. See *A Brief History of Time*, p. 44.

15. Ibid., p. 136. Emphasis added.

16. Ibid., pp. 135–6.

17. Ibid., pp. 137–8. Emphasis added.

18. Ibid., p. 138. Emphasis added.

19. 'Notizen zur Raumkonstitution', p. 226. Emphasis added.

20. Paul Virilio, *L'Horizon négatif*, Paris: Galilée, 1984.

INDEX

The letter n *following a page number indicates a reference in the notes*